Traditional Catholic Prayers

The 100 most inspiring and well-known prayers of the

Catholic religion

Anna Sophie Ashford

1. THE OUR FATHER (PATER NOSTER) 7
2. HAIL MARY (AVE MARIA) 8
3. THE CREED (OR THE APOSTLES' CREED)................................... 9
4. LE GLORIA 10
5. THE ACT OF CONTRITION... 11
6. THE BLESSINGS 12
7. THE MAGNIFICAT 13
8. THE CONFITEOR 14
9. THE AGNUS DEI (LAMB OF GOD) 15
10. KYRIE ELEISON (LORD, HAVE MERCY) 16
11. THE SANCTUS (HOLY, HOLY, HOLY).. 17
12. THE ANIMA CHRISTI (SOUL OF CHRIST) 18
13. THE PRAYER OF SAINT FRANCIS... 19
14. THE SALVE REGINA (HAIL, O QUEEN)....................................... 20
15. THE CHAPLET OF DIVINE MERCY 21
16. THE SERENITY PRAYER 22
17. THE NOVENA.. 23
18. THE PRAYER OF SAINT PATRICK (ARMOUR OF GOD)..................... 24
19. THE PRAYER OF SAINT THOMAS AQUINAS BEFORE STUDYING........... 27
20. PRAYERS OF BLESSING 28
21. HEALING PRAYERS 29
22. PRAYERS OF INTERCESSION 31
23. MORNING PRAYER (LAUDS) AND EVENING PRAYER (VESPERS) 33
24. THE MORNING OFFERING PRAYER 36
25. THE PRAYER OF SAINT IGNATIUS OF LOYOLA (TAKE, LORD, AND RECEIVE)37
26. THE PRAYER OF SAINT AUGUSTINE 38
27. THE PRAYER OF JABEZ (1 CHRONICLES 4:10)............................. 39
28. THE PRAYER OF SPIRITUAL COMMUNION 40
29. PRAYER OF CONSECRATION TO MARY 41
30. THE PRAYER OF SAINT MICHAEL THE ARCHANGEL....................... 42
31. PRAYERS FOR THE DEAD 43
32. EXAMINATION PRAYERS 45
33. PRAYERS BEFORE AND AFTER CONFESSION 46
34. THE ANGELUS PRAYER 47
35. SPOUSES' PRAYER 48
36. PRAYER OF THE ROSARY OF THE SEVEN SORROWS OF MARY 49
37. THE ROSARY OF SAINT JOSEPH 51
38. THE PRAYER OF SAINT THÉRÈSE OF LISIEUX 52

39. THE PRAYER OF SAINT GERTRUDE FOR THE SOULS IN PURGATORY 53
40. THE DIVINE MERCY PRAYER 54
41. THE PRAYER OF SAINT JOHN CHRYSOSTOM 56
42. THE PRAYER OF SAINT BRIGID 57
43. SAINT BENEDICT'S PRAYER OF PROTECTION 58
44. STATIONS OF THE CROSS (WAY OF THE CROSS) 59
45. THE PRAYER OF SAINT EPHREM THE SYRIAN 60
46. THE MISERERE (PSALM 51) 61
47. THE PRAYER OF SAINT CATHERINE OF SIENA 63
48. THE CHAPLET OF SAINT ANTHONY OF PADUA 64
49. THE REGINA COELI (QUEEN OF HEAVEN) 66
50. THE PRAYER OF SAINT BONAVENTURE 67
51. THE PRAYER OF SAINT EPHREM 68
52. THE CHAPLET OF DIVINE MERCY 69
53. THE PRAYER OF SAINT THOMAS MORE 71
54. THE TE DEUM 72
55. THE LITANIES OF THE SACRED HEART 74
56. THE ROSARY OF THE PRECIOUS BLOOD 76
57. THE PRAYER OF SAINT FRANCIS XAVIER 78
58. THE PRAYER OF SAINT BASIL THE GREAT 79
59. THE PRAYER OF SAINT ANSELM 80
60. THE PRAYER OF THE HEART 81
61. THE MAGNIFICAT 82
62. THE BENEDICTUS 83
63. THE NUNC DIMITTIS 85
64. THE ROSARY OF SAINT MICHAEL THE ARCHANGEL 86
65. THE PRAYER OF SAINT JOHN DAMASCENE 88
66. THE AKATHISTOS 89
67. THE CHAPLET OF THE DIVINE CHILDHOOD 90
68. THE PRAYER OF SAINT THOMAS AQUINAS AFTER COMMUNION 91
69. THE MORNING PRAYER OF SAINT PHILOMENA 92
70. THE LITANY OF SAINT JOSEPH 93
71. THE HOLY SPIRIT PRAYER OF SAINT TERESA OF AVILA 95
72. MORNING PRAYER TO THE HOLY TRINITY 96
73. THE LITANY OF THE HOLY CROSS 97
74. SAINT AUGUSTINE'S PRAYER TO THE HOLY TRINITY 99
75. THE PRAYER OF SAINT FRANÇOIS DE SALES 100
76. THE ROSARY OF THE VIRGIN MARY 101
77. THE PRAYER OF SAINT CLARE OF ASSISI 102

78. THE EVENING PRAYER OF SAINT BRIGID..............................103

79. THE ACT OF HOPE 104

80. PRAYER OF SAINT MONICA..............................105

81. SAINT ALPHONSUS DE LIGUORI'S PRAYER TO JESUS CRUCIFIED 106

82. SAINT BERNARD OF CLAIRVAUX'S PRAYER TO THE VIRGIN MARY (MEMORARE)..............................107

83. PRAYER OF SAINT RITA OF CASCIA..............................108

84. SAINT JOHN BOSCO'S PRAYER TO MARY HELP OF CHRISTIANS..........110

85. PRAYER OF SAINT JULIENNE OF NORWICH..............................111

86. SAINT MAXIMILIAN KOLBE'S PRAYER TO THE IMMACULATE CONCEPTION..............................112

87. PRAYER OF SAINT HILDEGARD OF BINGEN 113

88. SAINT JOHN PAUL II'S PRAYER TO MARY 114

89. SAINT JEROME'S PRAYER FOR THE STUDY OF SCRIPTURE..............115

90. PRAYER OF SAINT GERTRUDE FOR THE SOULS IN PURGATORY..........116

91. PRAYER OF SAINT MARGARET MARY ALACOQUE TO THE SACRED HEART OF JESUS..............................117

92. PRAYER OF SAINT JOHN OF THE CROSS..............................118

93. SAINT BENEDICT'S PRAYER FOR SEEKING GOD..............................119

94. PRAYER OF SAINT CECILIA..............................120

95. PRAYER OF SAINT THOMAS DE VILLENEUVE FOR CHARITY TOWARDS THE POOR..............................121

96. SAINT VINCENT DE PAUL'S PRAYER FOR LOVE OF NEIGHBOUR 122

97. PRAYER OF SAINT JEAN-MARIE VIANNEY 123

98. PRAYER OF SAINT ANTHONY OF PADUA..............................124

99. PRAYER OF SAINT MARTIN OF TOURS 125

100.   PRAYER OF SAINT CATHERINE OF SIENA 126

Welcome to this precious collection of prayers, where voices from the past and present meet to offer words of hope, devotion and gratitude. In this book, you will find a collection of the 100 best-known and most inspiring prayers from the Catholic tradition. Each of these prayers is a treasure that has spanned the centuries, touching countless hearts and influencing countless lives.

These prayers are more than just words. They are expressions of the deep faith and overwhelming love of those who created them. They offer us a glimpse into the spirituality of some of the Church's greatest saints, men and women who lived their lives in total dedication to God and to the service of others. In reading their prayers, we are invited to enter into their experience of God, to see the world through their eyes, and to share their deep desire for a deeper relationship with the divine.

Prayers by saints such as Saint Francis of Assisi, Saint Thérèse of Lisieux, Saint Augustine, and many others are included here, each prayer reflecting the uniqueness and spirituality of the person who composed it. These prayers are varied and diverse, but they all share a dedication to the love of God and an aspiration to holiness.

This book is intended to be a resource for personal prayer and meditation. You can read it cover to cover, or use it as a meditation book, reading and reflecting on one prayer at a time. Each prayer is accompanied by an introduction and conclusion, which provide context and reflection on the message of the prayer.

These prayers are an invitation to deepen your own relationship with God, to enter into the mystery of faith with an open heart and a willing soul. May they be a source of inspiration, comfort and spiritual renewal for you. May they guide you on your journey of faith, and help you to express your love for God and your desire to serve him.

Immerse yourself in these prayers with an open heart and a receptive mind. Let these words guide you on your own spiritual journey. May they help you find peace, comfort, and the infinite love of God who is always present with us. And may they be a reminder of the beauty and depth of the Catholic Church's tradition of prayer.

Glory to the father and the son and to the holy spirit

Three in one God, we offer our lives to you every day in the same way we close this prayer in the name of the father, and the son and of the holy spirit. Amen

Apostle Creed - our father
hail mary - Glory Be Be
Fatima prayer - Hail holy queen

1. The Our Father (Pater Noster)

This is probably the best-known Christian prayer. It was taught by Jesus to his disciples in the New Testament (Matthew 6:9-13 and Luke 11:2-4).

Our Father, who art in heaven,

Hallowed be thy name,

Thy kingdom come,

Thy will be done on earth as it is in heaven.

Give us this day our daily bread.

Forgive us our trespasses,

Just as we forgive those who offend us.

And lead us not into temptation

But deliver us from evil.

Amen.

It is a universal prayer found in almost all Christian traditions, whether Catholicism, Orthodoxy, Protestantism or Anglicanism. It covers several important themes, including the sanctification of God, the coming of God's kingdom, God's will, the request for daily sustenance, forgiveness of sins, and deliverance from temptation and evil.

2. Hail Mary (Ave Maria)

This prayer is mainly used in the Catholic tradition. It begins with the greetings of the angel Gabriel and Elizabeth to Mary in the Gospel of Luke, and ends with a request for prayer.

Hail Mary, full of grace,

The Lord is with you.

You are the most blessed of all women,

And blessed is the fruit of your womb, Jesus.

Holy Mary, Mother of God,

Pray for us sinners,

Now and at the hour of our death. Amen.

The first part of the prayer is taken directly from the Gospel of Luke in the New Testament, where the angel Gabriel greets Mary, announcing that she has been chosen to be the mother of the Messiah. The second part is an invocation of the Virgin Mary, asking her to intercede for believers both now and at the hour of their death.

3. The Creed (or the Ap

This is a statement of faith used in C
summarises fundamental Christian belief
Christ, the Holy Spirit, the Church and ete

I believe in God, the Father Almighty,
Creator of heaven and earth.
And in Jesus Christ, his only Son, our Lord,
who was conceived by the Holy Spirit,
was born of the Virgin Mary,
suffered under Pontius Pilate,
was crucified, died and was buried,
descended into hell,
rose from the dead on the third day,
ascended into heaven,
is seated at the right hand of God the Father Almighty,
from where he will come to judge the living and the dead.

I believe in the Holy Spirit,
to the Holy Catholic Church,
to the communion of saints,
the remission of sins,
to the resurrection of the flesh,
to eternal life. Amen.

The Creed is a summary of the Christian faith and the key
teachings of the Church. It covers many important aspects of
the faith, including belief in the Trinity (God the Father, Son
and Holy Spirit), the birth, death and resurrection of Jesus, the
holy Church, the communion of saints, the forgiveness of sins,
the resurrection of the dead and eternal life.

5. The Act of Contrition

This is a prayer of repentance, often said as part of the sacrament of reconciliation (or confession) in the Catholic tradition.

My God, I am very sorry to have offended You,

because You are infinitely good, infinitely kind,

and sin displeases you.

I firmly resolve to do so, with the help of Your holy grace,

to stop offending You and to do penance.

Amen.

There are several different versions of this prayer, but they all express the same fundamental feeling of contrition for the sins committed, love for God and resolution not to sin again in the future.

6. The Blessings

There are many blessings for different occasions, such as meals (the prayer before meals is often called "blessing" or "grace"), bedtime and various other occasions.

May the Lord bless you and keep you.

May the Lord make his face shine upon you and grant you his grace.

May the Lord turn his face towards you and give you peace.

Amen.

It should be noted that in Catholicism, certain specific blessings are reserved for priests and bishops. However, all Christians are called upon to bless others by praying for them and wishing them God's goodness.

Within the liturgy, the formula of blessing may vary according to the liturgical season (e.g. Advent, Lent, Easter, etc.) and the specific celebration.

There are also blessings for meals, often called "graces", which are prayed before or after meals to thank God for the food. Here is an example:

Bless us, O Lord, and these gifts which we are about to receive from your goodness, through Jesus Christ our Lord. Amen.

7. The Magnificat

This is the canticle of Mary, the mother of Jesus, which appears in the Gospel of Luke (Luke 1:46-55). It is attributed to Mary, the mother of Jesus, in response to the greeting of her cousin Elizabeth. In Latin, the first word of this hymn is "Magnificat", which means "he magnifies", hence the name of the prayer.

My soul praises the Lord,
My spirit rejoices in God, my Saviour!
He looked on his humble servant;
From now on, all ages will call me blessed.
The Mighty One did wonders for me;
Holy is his name!
His love extends from age to age
On those who fear him.
Deploying the strength of his arm,
It scatters the superb.
He topples the powerful from their thrones,
He lifts up the humble.
He fills the hungry with good things,
Send the rich away empty-handed.
He raises up Israel his servant,
He remembers his love,
The promise made to our fathers,
In favour of Abraham and his race for ever.
Gloria Patri, et Filio, et Spiritui Sancto,
Sicut erat in principio, et nunc, et semper, et in saecula saeculorum. Amen.

These words of Mary express her joy and gratitude to God for the honour he bestowed on her by choosing her to be the mother of the Saviour. The Magnificat is often recited or sung during the Liturgy of the Hours, particularly during Vespers (evening prayer).

8. The Confiteor

This is a prayer of confession of sins, often recited at Catholic Mass.

I confess to Almighty God,

I acknowledge before my brothers

that I have sinned in thought and word,

by action and omission ;

yes, I really have sinned.

That's why I'm begging the Virgin Mary,

the angels and all the saints,

and you too, my brothers,

to pray to the Lord our God for me.

By confessing their sins in this way, the faithful acknowledge that they need God's forgiveness and mercy. They also ask for the intercession of the Virgin Mary, the angels and the saints, as well as that of their brothers and sisters in the Christian community.

9. The Agnus Dei (Lamb of God)

This is a prayer recited during the Catholic Mass, just before communion, asking God to have mercy on us and to give us peace.

Lamb of God, who takes away the sin of the world, have mercy on us.

Lamb of God, who takes away the sin of the world, have mercy on us.

Lamb of God, who takes away the sin of the world, give us peace.

In this prayer, Jesus is referred to as the "Lamb of God", a title that refers to his sacrifice on the cross for the salvation of the world. The faithful ask for God's mercy and peace.

It should be noted that the phrase "who takes away the sin of the world" recalls the testimony of John the Baptist when he saw Jesus coming towards him: "Behold the Lamb of God, who takes away the sin of the world" (John 1:29).

10. Kyrie Eleison (Lord, have mercy)

This short prayer is used in the Orthodox and Catholic liturgies, asking for God's mercy.

Kyrie Eleison,

Christe Eleison,

Kyrie Eleison.

The use of Greek for this prayer, even in liturgies otherwise celebrated in Latin or the vernacular, is a reminder of the Eastern roots of Christianity. The "Kyrie" prayer expresses an appeal to God's mercy and love for humanity. It is traditionally sung or recited at the beginning of Mass, after the Confiteor, as part of the penitential act.

11. The Sanctus (Holy, Holy, Holy)

This is part of the Eucharistic liturgy in many Christian denominations, which praises God and proclaims him as holy.

Holy, holy, holy, the Lord, God of the universe.

Heaven and earth are full of your glory.

Hosanna in the highest heaven.

Blessed is he who comes in the name of the Lord.

Hosanna in the highest heaven.

The Sanctus is an acclamation of God's holiness and a praise of His glory. It is often sung by the congregation, and is one of the highlights of the Eucharistic liturgy.

The term "Hosanna" is an exclamation of joy and prayer for salvation that appears in the accounts of Jesus' triumphal entry into Jerusalem in the New Testament Gospels. "Blessed is he who comes in the name of the Lord" is a quotation from Psalm 118, and it was taken up by the crowd as Jesus entered Jerusalem.

12. The Anima Christi (Soul of Christ)

This is a traditional Catholic prayer asking for Jesus' help and presence.

The "Anima Christi", or "Soul of Christ", is a traditional Catholic prayer of devotion to Jesus. It is often recited after receiving communion, although it is not officially part of the liturgy of the Mass. Here is the text of the prayer:

Soul of Christ, sanctify me.
Body of Christ, save me.
Blood of Christ, intoxicate me.
Water from the side of Christ, wash me.
Passion of Christ, strengthen me.
O good Jesus, hear me.
Hide me in your wounds.
Don't let me be separated from you.
Defend me from the evil enemy.
When I die, call me.
And command me to come to you,
So that with your saints I may praise you,
For ever and ever. Amen.

This prayer expresses a desire for deeper communion with Jesus and asks for His protection and help. The references to the soul, body, blood and water of Christ's side recall the mysteries of the Passion and the Eucharist.

15. The Chaplet of Divine Mercy

This is a special devotion in the Catholic Church, inspired by the visions of Saint Faustina Kowalska, a Polish nun. In these visions, which she recorded in her "Little Diary", Jesus himself is said to have given instructions for this prayer.

The Divine Mercy Chaplet is often recited on a standard rosary of five decades, similar to that used for the Rosary. Here is the structure of the prayer:

1. Begin with the "Our Father", the "Hail Mary" and the "Creed".

2. On the large beads (normally reserved for the "Our Father" in the Rosary), say: "Eternal Father, I offer you the Body, Blood, Soul and Divinity of your Beloved Son, Our Lord Jesus Christ, in reparation for our sins and those of the whole world".

3. On the small beads (normally reserved for the "Hail Mary" in the Rosary), say: "Through his painful Passion, be merciful to us and to the whole world".

4. Conclude by repeating three times: "Holy God, Strong God, Eternal God, have mercy on us and on the whole world".

Devotion to the Divine Mercy focuses on God's mercy towards sinners and encourages the faithful to entrust themselves to this mercy. It is particularly associated with the Feast of Divine Mercy, which is celebrated on the Sunday following Easter.

16. The Serenity Prayer

Although not specifically Christian in origin, this prayer has been widely adopted by many Christian communities. It calls for serenity, courage and wisdom to face life's challenges.

"My goodness,

give me serenity

to accept the things I can't change,

the courage to change the things I can,

and the wisdom to know the difference."

There are longer versions of this prayer, but it is generally this abbreviated version that is the best known and most widely used.

The Serenity Prayer was originally written in English by the American theologian Reinhold Niebuhr in the mid-20th century. It has since been translated into many languages and is used in a variety of contexts, both religious and secular.

17. The Novena

In the Catholic tradition, a novena is a series of prayers said over nine consecutive days, usually asking for a specific grace or in honour of a particular saint.

Novenas are often undertaken to ask for a special grace, the intercession of a saint, or as preparation for an important religious feast. There are many different novenas, each with a specific intention or patron saint. For example, the novena to Saint Joseph, the novena to Saint Thérèse of Lisieux, the novena to the Sacred Heart of Jesus, etc.

Here is an example of a daily prayer in the Novena to Saint Joseph:

"O Saint Joseph, whose protection is so great, so strong, so prompt before the throne of God, I place in you all my hopes and all my affairs. O Saint Joseph, assist me by your powerful intercession and obtain for me from your divine Son all spiritual blessings through Jesus Christ, our Lord, so that, having engaged your heavenly power here below, I may offer you my thanks and gratitude. O Saint Joseph, I never tire of contemplating you and Jesus asleep in your arms. I dare not approach you while He rests close to your heart. Kiss Him in my name, and ask Him to come back to me when I wake up, He will find me close to Him. Amen."

Each day of the novena, this prayer is generally followed by specific prayers or requests linked to the particular intention of the person doing the novena.

18. The Prayer of Saint Patrick
(Armour of God)

This prayer, attributed to Saint Patrick, the patron saint of Ireland, is an invocation of divine protection.

"I rise today
By a powerful force, the invocation of the Trinity,
Through faith in Threeness,
Through the confession of Unity
of the Creator of creation.

I rise today
Through the power of Christ's birth with His baptism,
By the power of His crucifixion and death,
By the power of His resurrection with His ascension,
By the force of His descent for the Final Judgement.

I rise today
By the power of the cherubim's love,
In obedience to the angels,
In the service of the archangels,
In the hope of the resurrection to obtain the reward,
In the prayers of the patriarchs,
In the predictions of the prophets,
In the preaching of the apostles,
In the faith of confessors,
In the innocence of holy virgins,
In the actions of righteous men.

I rise today
By the power of heaven :
Sunlight,
Brightness of the moon,

The splendour of fire,
Lightning speed,
Wind speed,
Depth of the sea,
Stability of the earth,
Rock solidity.

I rise today
With God's strength to guide me,
The power of God to sustain me,
God's wisdom to guide me,
The eye of God to see before me,
God's ear to hear me,
The word of God to speak for me,
The hand of God to keep me,
God's path set out before me,
God's shield to protect me,
God's army to save me from the temptation of demons,
From everyone who wishes me ill,
Far and near,
Alone and in multitudes.

May Christ protect me today
Against poison, against burning,
Against drowning, against injury,
So that I can receive a multitude of awards.
Christ be with me, Christ before me, Christ behind me,
Christ in me, Christ beneath me, Christ above me,
Christ on my right, Christ on my left,
Christ when I lie down, Christ when I sit down, Christ when
I get up,
Christ in the heart of every man who thinks of me,
Christ in the mouth of every man who speaks of me,
Christ in every eye that sees me,

Christ in every ear that hears me.

I rise today
By a powerful force, the invocation of the Trinity,
Through faith in Threeness,
Through the confession of Unity
of the Creator of creation.
Amen."

It's a powerful prayer invoking God's protection and help for the day ahead, with a deep recognition of God's presence in all aspects of life.

19.   The Prayer of Saint Thomas Aquinas before studying

This prayer is often used by Christian students seeking divine help for their learning and understanding.

"Ineffable Creator,

You are the true source of light and wisdom,

deign to shed a ray of your light on the darkness of my mind.

Give me the penetrating intelligence to understand,

sufficient capacity to retain,

a method and ease of learning,

the subtlety to interpret,

and an abundance of graces to speak of.

Make me walk in the path of truth,

and that I am so purified by the teaching of this doctrine,

that I will never be convicted.

Amen."

This prayer is a beautiful request for clarity, understanding and wisdom, and it reflects Saint Thomas Aquinas' profound respect for the power of the human intellect and the need to illuminate it with God's grace.

20. Prayers of Blessing

These prayers are often said by a priest or other religious leader to bless people, places or objects.

In the Christian tradition, a blessing is generally accompanied by the sign of the cross. The priest or deacon makes the sign of the cross over the object of the blessing while reciting the prayer.

Blessing of a house :
"Lord God of goodness and mercy, we ask You to bless this house and all those who live in it. May Your love and peace dwell here. In Thy name we consecrate this house to Thee. Amen."

Blessing of a meal :
"Bless us, O Lord, and bless this meal we are about to eat. Give bread to the hungry and give us a hunger for justice. Amen."

Blessing of a child :
"God, our Father, we entrust this child to you. Bless him (her) and guide him (her) on the path of life. May Your love envelop him (her) always and may he (she) grow in wisdom and grace. Amen."

Blessing before a journey:
"Lord, we ask You to protect us on our journey. Guide us and keep us safe. May your angel accompany us and protect us. Amen."

There are prayers of blessing for almost every occasion. These prayers are a way of inviting God into every aspect of our lives and dedicating our actions to His glory.

21. Healing Prayers

These prayers ask God to heal the sick or relieve suffering.

Prayers for healing are a form of prayer often used in Christian traditions, asking God to intervene and provide physical, emotional or spiritual healing for someone who is ill or suffering. These prayers can be said by the person in need of healing, or by others on their behalf. Here are some examples of healing prayers:

Prayer for general healing :

"Lord God, we ask you to intervene in [name]'s life. You are the Great Physician and we believe in your healing power. Touch [name] with Your healing hand, ease his pain and restore his strength. Give him peace and patience in this time of trial. We entrust [name] to You and ask that You heal him according to Your will. Amen."

Prayer for emotional healing :

"Loving God, you know the heart and mind of [name]. You see the pain and distress that overwhelm him. We ask you to send your Holy Spirit to heal him. Fill him with your peace, comfort him in his grief, help him forgive those who have hurt him, and bring him healing from all emotional trauma. Amen."

Prayer for spiritual healing :

"Almighty God, we ask you to intervene in the spiritual life

of [name]. Free him from all bonds of sin, guide him along the path of holiness and bring him closer to You. Restore his faith in You and help him to live according to Your commandments. May Your love and mercy guide him to full spiritual healing. Amen."

It is important to remember that although we often ask for physical healing in these prayers, the most important thing is spiritual healing, and that all suffering can be used to bring us closer to God. We should never stop asking God for guidance and help, even in times of illness or difficulty.

22. Prayers of Intercession

These prayers ask God to intervene and help others.

Intercessory prayer is a form of Christian prayer in which we implore God for the needs of others. Instead of focusing on one's own needs or desires, the pray-er seeks to use his or her prayer as a means of bringing the burdens of others before God.

These prayers can be offered for specific individuals, for groups of people, or for the whole world. They can concern all kinds of issues, such as illness, poverty, conflict, injustice, and much more.

Here are some examples of intercessory prayers:

Intercessory prayer for peace in the world :

"Lord, we pray to you for peace in the world. May you bring reconciliation where there is conflict, may you bring healing where there is hatred and resentment. Guide the leaders of nations to seek the common good and justice. Amen."

Intercessory prayer for the sick :

"Loving and merciful God, we bring to You in our prayers all those who suffer from illness, whether physical, mental or spiritual. We ask You to enfold them in Your love, to comfort them in their pain and to bring them healing according to Your will. Amen."

Intercessory prayer for the poor and marginalised :

"Lord, we pray to You for all those who live in poverty,

oppression or marginalisation. Open our hearts to their needs and give us the will to act for justice. Help us to share generously the gifts you have entrusted to us, so that all may know your goodness and love. Amen."

Prayers of intercession are a powerful way of putting our faith into action, inviting God to act in the world and expressing our solidarity with those who suffer. They are a tangible expression of Christian love for our neighbour.

23. Morning Prayer (Lauds) and Evening Prayer (Vespers)

They form part of the Liturgy of the Hours recited by monks, nuns and some lay people.

Morning prayer (Lauds) and evening prayer (Vespers) are part of the Liturgy of the Hours, also known as the Divine Office. This is the daily prayer cycle of the Roman Catholic Church and many other Christian traditions. The Liturgy of the Hours is intended to sanctify the day and is mainly recited by clerics and nuns, but lay people are also encouraged to recite it.

Lauds are usually recited at sunrise or at the beginning of the day. They are intended to consecrate the day's journey to God and to prepare it in prayer. A typical Lauds consists of a hymn, one or more psalms, a short reading from the Bible, a hymn of praise (usually the Song of Zechariah), intercessions, the Lord's Prayer and a concluding prayer.

Vespers is usually recited at sunset or at the end of the day. They are intended to thank God for the day gone by and to ask for his protection during the night ahead. A typical Vespers consists of a hymn, one or more psalms, a short reading from the Bible, a hymn of praise (usually the Canticle of Mary or Magnificat), intercessions, the Our Father and a concluding prayer.

It is important to note that the Liturgy of the Hours varies according to the liturgical season (for example, Advent, Lent, Ordinary Time, etc.) and specific feasts. As a result, the psalms and specific readings change from day to day. However, the general format remains the same. There are books and applications that provide the specific texts for each day.

Example of Lauds (Morning Prayer) :

Introduction: **"O God, come to my aid; Lord, help me quickly. Glory be to the Father, and to the Son, and to the Holy Spirit, to the God who is and who was and who is to come for ever and ever. Amen. Hallelujah."**

Hymn: [This can vary, but is usually a song or psalm of worship. For example, Psalm 63]

Psalm: [This varies from day to day, for example, Psalm 95, the Invitatory Psalm].

Short Bible reading: [This varies from day to day].

Song: The Song of Zechariah (Luke 1:68-79)

Intercessions: [These vary from day to day and are usually linked to the readings or festivals of the day].

Our Father.

Concluding Prayer: **"Lord our God, you who have already poured out the light of your wisdom at daybreak, show yourself to our minds and hearts even now; may we learn to know you and love you with all our strength, and so come to the blessed vision in your light. Through Jesus Christ, our Lord. Amen."**

Example of Vespers (Evening Prayer) :

Introduction: **"God, help me, Lord, help us. Glory be to the Father, and to the Son, and to the Holy Spirit, for ever and ever. Amen."**

Hymn: [This can vary, but is usually a song or psalm of praise. For example, Psalm 141]

Psalm: [It varies from day to day].

Short Bible reading: [This varies from day to day].

Song: The Magnificat (Luke 1:46-55)

Intercessions: [These vary from day to day and are usually linked to the readings or festivals of the day].

Our Father.

Concluding prayer: **"Lord, source of all goodness, who has brought us to the end of this day, grant that we may spend this night in peace, so that at daybreak we may be more eager to serve you. Through Jesus Christ, our Lord. Amen."**

Note: The psalms, readings and intercessions vary from day to day, so these examples are very general. The specific texts for each day can be found in a prayer book or an application of the Liturgy of the Hours.

24. The Morning Offering Prayer

It's a prayer that offers God the actions of the day ahead.

The Morning Offering Prayer is a Christian prayer that consists of offering the day ahead to God. It can vary from one tradition to another and from one person to another, but it generally aims to consecrate all the actions, joys, sufferings and experiences of the day to God. Here is an example of a Morning Offering Prayer:

"My God, I offer you this day. I offer you my prayers, my works, my joys and my sorrows. Grant me the grace to do everything for your glory, to avoid anything that might displease you and to always seek you first. Help me to live this day aware of your presence in me and in those around me. May everything I do today be for your glory. Amen."

This prayer is a way of starting the day by remembering God's presence and dedicating ourselves to his will. It can be recited on its own or as a complement to other morning prayers, such as Lauds in the Liturgy of the Hours.

25. The Prayer of Saint Ignatius of Loyola (Take, Lord, and receive)

This prayer is often associated with Ignatian spirituality and spiritual discernment. It is an act of total abandonment to God.

The Prayer of Saint Ignatius of Loyola, also known as the "Generosity Prayer", is one of the best-known prayers attributed to this saint. Here is the prayer:

"Lord, teach me to be generous,

to serve you as you deserve,

to give without counting the cost,

to fight without worrying about injuries,

working without resting,

to spend myself without expecting any other reward

that of knowing that I am doing your holy will.

Amen."

It is a prayer that expresses a desire for total dedication to God and selfless service to others, two key values of Ignatian spirituality. It is often used in retreats and spiritual formation programmes inspired by the Jesuit tradition.

It should be noted that Saint Ignatius of Loyola is also known for the Spiritual Exercises, an intensive programme of prayer and meditation designed to help people discern God's will for their lives. This programme includes many other prayers and spiritual practices.

26. The Prayer of Saint Augustine

(Tarde te amavi - "Late I loved you")

This prayer by Saint Augustine, taken from his Confessions, expresses deep gratitude for God's love.

"Late have I loved thee, O Beauty so ancient and so new, late have I loved thee!

And you were inside and I was outside.

And there I was looking for you, and for the grace of the things you have done,

Wretch that I was, I rushed!

You were with me and I wasn't with you.

They kept me away from you, these things that nevertheless..,

If they weren't inside you, they wouldn't exist.

You called, you shouted, and you broke my deafness.

You shone and shone and dispelled my blindness.

You embalmed, I breathed and gasped for you.

I've tasted it, and I'm hungry and thirsty.

You touched me, and I was inflamed by your peace."

This prayer is a reflection of Saint Augustine's conversion experience and expresses the joy of discovering God's love after having long sought happiness in the things of the world. It is often cited as an example of the intimacy with God that can be achieved through prayer and spiritual reflection.

27. The Prayer of Jabez (1 Chronicles 4:10)

This prayer from the Old Testament asks God to bless, to enlarge territories, to keep from evil and to cause no pain.

The Prayer of Jabez is a short but powerful prayer found in the Old Testament of the Bible, specifically in 1 Chronicles 4:10. Jabez is a biblical character who, despite only one mention in the Bible, left a significant legacy through his prayer. Here is the prayer:

"And Jabez called upon the God of Israel, saying: Oh that you would bless me and enlarge my land! May your hand be with me and keep me from evil, so that I will not be in pain! And God granted what he had asked for."

This prayer reflects Jabez's trust in God to bless, protect and extend his territory. In other words, Jabez asked God to grant him prosperity, protection and God's presence in his life. This prayer became more popular through the book "The Prayer of Jabez: Unlocking the Secret of God's Blessing" by Bruce Wilkinson, where the author encourages readers to pray like Jabez for God's blessing and protection.

28. The Prayer of Spiritual Communion

This prayer is often used by those who cannot receive the Eucharist at Mass, but who still wish to receive Christ spiritually.

The Prayer for Spiritual Communion is a traditional Christian prayer that expresses the desire to receive Jesus Christ in Holy Communion, especially in situations where it is not possible to receive the Eucharist physically. Here is an example of this prayer:

"My Jesus,
I believe that you are present in the Blessed Sacrament.
I love you more than anything,
And I want to receive you into my soul.
I can't receive you sacramentally now,
At least come spiritually into my heart.
I kiss you as if you were already here,
And I am completely united with you.
Never let me be separated from you.
Amen."

This prayer can be said during Mass when physical communion is not possible, or at any other time to express the desire for union with Jesus. It is particularly used by those who are unable to attend Mass in person for reasons of health, distance or other constraints.

29. Prayer of Consecration to Mary

This prayer is an act of personal consecration to the Virgin Mary, often associated with Saint Louis de Montfort or Saint Maximilien Kolbe.

The Prayer of Consecration to Mary is a prayer dedicated to the Virgin Mary, the mother of Jesus. In this prayer, the faithful offer their life, heart and soul to Mary, and ask for her intercession and protection. There are many versions of this prayer, of which the Prayer of Consecration to the Virgin Mary by Saint Louis-Marie Grignion de Montfort is particularly well known. Here is the prayer:

"I choose you today, O Mary, in the presence of the whole heavenly court, to be my Mother and my Queen. I surrender and consecrate to you, in all submission and love, my body and soul, my inner and outer possessions, and the very value of my good deeds past, present and future, leaving you a full and complete right to dispose of me, and all that belongs to me, without exception, according to your good pleasure, to the greater glory of God, in time and in eternity. Amen."

This prayer is often recited by those who follow a Marian devotion, and can be said every day, or on special Marian feasts and celebrations. It is also often associated with the act of wearing a scapular or a miraculous medal, as a sign of commitment to live according to Mary's example of faith and love.

30. The Prayer of Saint Michael the Archangel

This prayer asks Saint Michael for protection against evil.

The Prayer of Saint Michael the Archangel is a traditional Catholic prayer asking for the assistance and protection of Saint Michael. This prayer was written by Pope Leo XIII in the 19th century. Here is the prayer:

"Saint Michael the Archangel,

defend us in battle,

be our help against the devil's malice and ambushes.

May God exercise his empire over him, we beseech you.

And you, Prince of the Celestial Militia,

pushed back into hell by divine force,

Satan and the other evil spirits lurking in the world

to lose souls.

Amen."

Saint Michael is known in the Bible as the leader of the heavenly armies who defeated Satan in the heavenly war (Revelation 12:7-9). He is often invoked for protection against evil and the forces of evil. This prayer was particularly used during the rites of exorcism and is sometimes recited at the end of Mass.

31. Prayers for the Dead

These prayers are used to ask for eternal rest for those who have died and to console those who mourn.

Prayers for the dead are an important part of Christian tradition. They are intended to ask God to give rest to the souls of the dead and to welcome them into eternal life. Here is an example of a prayer for the dead:

"Almighty and eternal God,
You who are the resurrection and the life,
we pray for your servant [name of the deceased].
that you have called back from this world of yours.
Forgive him/her his/her sins
and grant her eternal joy in the light of your countenance.
Through Jesus, the Christ, our Lord.
Amen."

There is also the **"Requiem Aeternam"**, a traditional Latin prayer for the dead:

"Requiem aeternam dona eis, Domine,

et lux perpetua luceat eis.

Requiescant in pace.

Amen."

This translates into :

"Eternal rest grant unto them, O Lord,

and let perpetual light shine on them.

May they rest in peace.

Amen."

These prayers can be recited at funerals, masses for the dead, visits to the cemetery, or simply as a personal prayer for a loved one who has died.

32. Examination Prayers

These prayers are often used at the end of the day to review the day's events in God's presence. This is a common practice in Ignatian spirituality.

Examination of conscience is a traditional prayer practice in Christianity, particularly in the Ignatian tradition (Saint Ignatius of Loyola, the founder of the Jesuits). It involves taking a moment each day to reflect on our actions and thoughts with the aim of growing spiritually and becoming closer to God. Here is an example of an Examen prayer:

"Lord, I thank You for all the gifts You have given me today. I ask You to help me see how I have responded to Your love throughout the day.

I ask the Holy Spirit for help in knowing my sins and recognising my weaknesses. Where have I failed today? Where have I been selfish or lacking in charity towards those I meet?

Lord, help me to see how I can grow and improve tomorrow. Give me the courage to ask for forgiveness and the desire to become closer to you.

I ask this grace in the name of Jesus, our Lord. Amen."

An examination of conscience is recommended at the end of the day, but it can be done at any time. It helps us not only to identify sins and areas for improvement, but also to recognise and appreciate the moments of grace and blessing in our daily lives.

33. Prayers before and after Confession

These prayers help to prepare the heart before confessing sins and to express gratitude after receiving God's forgiveness.

Confession, also known as the sacrament of penance or reconciliation, is an important sacrament in the Catholic Church where the faithful confess their sins to a priest to receive absolution. There are specific prayers that can be recited before and after confession to help prepare and express gratitude for the forgiveness of sins.

Before confession, you can pray a prayer of examination of conscience, as mentioned above. Here is an example of a prayer before confession:

"Lord, help me to make a good confession. Enlighten me so that I can recognise my sins. Help me to detach myself sincerely from all my faults out of love for you. Give me the courage and the will to correct myself and to avoid all occasions of sin in the future. Amen."

After confession, we can express our gratitude for the forgiveness of sins and the grace received with a prayer of thanksgiving. Here is an example of a prayer after confession:

"My God, I thank you for forgiving me and renewing me with your love and mercy. Help me to live a new life in the image of your Son, Jesus. Grant me the grace not to fall back into my past sins, but to grow in holiness and love for you and for my neighbours. Amen."

34. The Angelus Prayer

This traditional prayer is often recited three times a day (morning, noon and evening), and focuses on the Incarnation of Jesus.

The Angelus is a traditional Christian prayer in honour of the Annunciation, the biblical event when the angel Gabriel announced to Mary that she would conceive and give birth to Jesus. This prayer is usually recited three times a day: at six in the morning, at midday and at six in the evening. Here is the Angelus:

The angel of the Lord brought the news to Mary.
And she conceived of the Holy Spirit.
Hail Mary, full of grace...
Behold the handmaid of the Lord.
Let it be done to me according to your word.
Hail Mary, full of grace...
And the Word became flesh.
And he dwelt among us.
Hail Mary, full of grace...
Pray for us, holy Mother of God.
That we may be worthy of the promises of Christ.
Let us pray. Lord, pour your grace into our hearts: having known, through the Angel's message, the incarnation of your beloved Son, we come, through his passion and his cross, to the glory of his resurrection. Through the same Jesus Christ, our Lord. Amen.

It's a beautiful way to remember God's Incarnation throughout the day, and to pause for prayer and reflection, even in the midst of daily activities.

35. Spouses' Prayer

There are various prayers that couples can say together, asking God to bless their union and help them to love and support their partner.

The spouses' prayer is a prayer that married couples can say together to ask God to bless them and guide them in their marriage. Here is an example of a spouses' prayer:

"Lord, we thank You for Your love and Your presence in our marriage. Help us always to love each other with the same love that You have shown us by uniting us in the sacrament of marriage.

Help us to be patient and understanding with each other, to forgive as you forgive us, and to always seek the good of the other before our own.

Give us the wisdom and strength to resist temptations and overcome the challenges we face in our marriage. Make our home a place of love, peace and joy.

Bless us in our love and make us grow in love and fidelity every day of our lives. May our marriage be a testimony to your love and fidelity.

We ask this through Jesus Christ, our Lord. Amen."

This prayer can be adapted to meet the specific needs of the couple, and it is recommended that it be said regularly to nourish and strengthen the marital commitment.

36. Prayer of the Rosary of the Seven Sorrows of Mary

This form of the Rosary focuses on the seven sufferings that the Virgin Mary underwent in her life, linked to the sufferings of her son Jesus.

The Rosary of the Seven Sorrows of Mary is a traditional Catholic devotion that commemorates the seven sorrows or afflictions of the Virgin Mary in her life, as recorded in the Bible. This prayer is a meditation on Mary's compassion and her participation in the suffering of her son Jesus. This is how the Rosary of the Seven Sorrows is usually prayed:

We begin by saying "Hail Mary" three times in memory of the tears Mary shed because of her love for her son Jesus.

Then each of the Seven Sorrows is announced, meditating on each event and praying an "Our Father" and seven "Hail Marys".

The Seven Sorrows are :

The prophecy of Simeon (Luke 2:34-35)

The flight into Egypt (Matthew 2:13-21)

The loss of the Child Jesus in the temple (Luke 2:41-52)

The meeting of Mary and Jesus on the road to Calvary (Luke 23:27-31)

Mary contemplating Jesus on the cross (John 19:25-27)

Mary receives the body of Jesus from the cross (Matthew 27:57-61)

The burial of Jesus (John 19:40-42)

At the end of the prayer, the "Hail Mary" is recited three times in memory of Mary's tears and the pain she felt at the death of Jesus.

This prayer is a way of connecting more deeply with Christ's passion through the experience of his mother, and it can be particularly powerful during Lent and Holy Week.

37. The Rosary of Saint Joseph

A traditional Catholic devotional prayer in honour of Saint Joseph, the adoptive father of Jesus.

The Rosary of Saint Joseph is a Catholic prayer dedicated to Saint Joseph, the adoptive father of Jesus. This prayer is often recited to ask for Saint Joseph's intercession for a particular cause or in honour of his holiness and his role in salvation history. This is how the Rosary of Saint Joseph is usually prayed:

The Saint Joseph rosary is made up of 15 groups of 4 beads each, separated by a large bead. The 15 groups represent the 15 joyful, sorrowful and glorious mysteries of Saint Joseph's life.

Begin each decade with the following prayer:

"In the name of the Father, and of the Son, and of the Holy Spirit. Amen. Jesus, Mary and Joseph, I give you my heart and my soul (on the large pearl)".

Then, on each group of 4 beads, recite :
"Jesus, Mary and Joseph, help me in my last battles (on the four little pearls)".
After each decade, recite :
"Jesus, Mary and Joseph, may my soul expire in peace among you. (On the great pearl)"
At the end of the rosary, recite the following invocation:

"A grace, Saint Joseph, a grace: it is from you that I ask it; in your goodness, you cannot refuse me. Amen."

The Rosary of Saint Joseph is a wonderful way of meditating on the life of the saint and asking for his intercession.

38. The Prayer of Saint Thérèse of Lisieux

Saint Thérèse of Lisieux, also known as Thérèse of the Child Jesus, was renowned for her "little way" of spirituality. Her philosophy was to do the little things in life with great love, rather than seeking to do great deeds but without love. She believed that it is in these small daily actions done with love that we come closer to God.

A well-known prayer of Saint Thérèse of Lisieux is the following:

"My God, I offer you all the actions I am going to do today, in the intentions and for the glory of Jesus Christ, I want to sanctify the beating of my heart, my thoughts, my simplest works by uniting them to his infinite merits; and to make reparation for my faults I offer you all the pain I am going to endure, amen."

It is important to note that this prayer represents the philosophy of Thérèse's "little way": to offer every action, every thought and every suffering to God, no matter how insignificant they may seem. Thérèse believed that by doing this we could truly live a life consecrated to God.

39. The Prayer of Saint Gertrude for the Souls in Purgatory

This prayer is often recited to ask for the release of souls in Purgatory.

The prayer of Saint Gertrude for the souls in Purgatory is a prayer that Saint Gertrude the Great is said to have received from Jesus in a vision. This prayer has traditionally been used to pray for the souls of those in Purgatory, asking God to free them from their suffering and welcome them into heaven. Here is the prayer:

"Eternal Father, I offer You the most precious Blood of Your Divine Son, Jesus, in union with the Masses celebrated today throughout the world, for all the holy souls in Purgatory, for sinners everywhere, for sinners in the universal Church, those in my own home and family. Amen."

It is a simple but powerful prayer that emphasises the importance of God's mercy and forgiveness. It is important to note that, although this prayer is traditionally associated with the release of souls from purgatory, it can be prayed by anyone seeking to ask God for mercy and forgiveness for themselves or others.

40. The Divine Mercy Prayer

This prayer asks God to show his mercy to the world.

The Divine Mercy Prayer, also known as the Chaplet of Divine Mercy, was revealed by Jesus to Saint Faustina Kowalska, a Polish nun, in the 20th century. Jesus asked Saint Faustina to spread the message of his mercy throughout the world. The prayer is usually recited using a rosary. This is how it is usually prayed:

Start by making the sign of the cross.

Then, on the "first three beads" of the rosary, recite the Our Father, the Hail Mary and the Creed.

On the "grains of the Our Father", recite: **"Eternal Father, I offer You the Body and Blood, Soul and Divinity of Your beloved Son, Our Lord Jesus Christ, in reparation for our sins and those of the whole world"**.

On the "grains of the Hail Mary", recite: **"Through His sorrowful Passion, have mercy on us and on the whole world"**.

Repeat these prayers for each decade of the rosary.

At the end of the rosary, recite three times: **"Holy God, Strong God, Immortal God, have mercy on us and on the whole world"**.

Finally, end with this prayer: **"O Eternal God, in the Treasure of Compassion which is inexhaustible, look upon us with kindness and multiply Your mercy in us, so that in difficult times we may not despair or lose heart, but may always trust and lovingly surrender to Your holy will,**

which is Love and Mercy itself".

Let's remember that this prayer, like all prayers, is not a magic formula, but rather a way of opening our hearts to God and asking for his mercy.

41. The Prayer of Saint John Chrysostom

This prayer asks for God's help in leading a life of righteousness and virtue.

Saint John Chrysostom, a 4th-century bishop, is one of the most famous Church Fathers and is particularly well known for his eloquence in preaching and liturgy. He wrote many prayers and homilies that are still used in the Orthodox Church and the Catholic Church today.

One of his best-known prayers is the following:

"O Lord, master of my life, remove from me the spirit of laziness, discouragement, domination and idle chatter. But give your servant the spirit of chastity, humility, patience and love. Yes, Lord King, give me to see my own faults and not to judge my brother, for you are blessed for ever and ever. Amen."

In this prayer, Saint John Chrysostom asks God to help him overcome sins and temptations and to cultivate the virtues of humility, patience and love. He also asks for the grace to be able to see one's own faults rather than judging others, an important lesson for all Christians.

It is a deeply humble prayer that recognises our constant need for God's mercy and grace. It can be said in any circumstance where we feel the need for greater humility and patience, and a greater capacity to love others.

42. The Prayer of Saint Brigid

Saint Brigid of Sweden had a series of visions that inspired prayers dedicated to the wounds of Jesus.

Saint Brigid of Sweden was a mystic and saint of the 14th century. She is best known for the revelations she received from God, many of which were recorded in her writings. Among these revelations is a set of prayers known as the "Prayers of Saint Brigid" or "The 15 Oraisons of Saint Brigid". These prayers are usually prayed for a whole year and focus on the Passion of Christ.

Here is an example of one of these prayers:

"I beg You with the greatest fervour to deign to imprint in my heart sentiments of faith, hope and charity, true regret for my sins and a firm intention to amend myself, while I meditate within myself and mentally make the details of Your holy Passion".

"O Jesus! I beg You, through the memory of this path which You trod all covered in blood, to forgive me for all the sins I have committed, from the day I began to offend Your divine Majesty until now, for all those I intend to commit in the future, and for all those I have neglected to confess. May the thought of these sins fill me with such contrition and self-loathing that I may never commit them again in the future. I love You, O my God, more than myself, and I regret with all my heart having offended You. I propose to die rather than offend You any more. So be it."

This prayer, like all the Prayers of Saint Brigid, focuses on humility, repentance for sins, and love for God and for others.

43. Saint Benedict's Prayer of Protection

This prayer invokes the protection of Saint Benedict, known for his piety and miracles.

Saint Benedict's Prayer of Protection is a powerful example of a prayer of intercession and protection. Saint Benedict, the founder of the Benedictine monastic order, is renowned for his efforts to protect against evil and for his dedication to a life of prayer and work.

The Medal of Saint Benedict, which bears a prayer for protection, is often used as a reminder of this prayer and of the protection that Saint Benedict offers. The words on the medal in Latin are :

V.R.S.N.S.M.V - S.M.Q.L.I.V.B
C.S.P.B. - C.S.S.M.L. - N.D.S.M.D., P.P.S.
Which means:

"Vade retro Satana! Nunquam suade mihi vana!
Sunt mala quae libas. Ipse venena bibas!
Crux sacra sit mihi lux! Nunquam draco sit mihi dux!
Pax vobiscum."
This translates into :
"Begone, Satan! You'll never persuade me of anything vain.
You're offering me evil, so drink your own poisons.
Let the sacred cross be my light! Let not the dragon be my guide.
Peace be with you."
This prayer is an invocation to God for protection against evil and a strong declaration of faith in God and the protection He offers.

44. Stations of the Cross (Way of the Cross)

Although it is more a rite than a single prayer, the Way of the Cross consists of prayers and meditations on the last hours of Jesus' life.

Stations of the Cross, also known as the Way of the Cross, are a traditional devotion observed by many Christians, particularly Catholics. They commemorate the last hours of Jesus' life, from his condemnation to his crucifixion and burial. There are traditionally fourteen stations, although some traditions include fifteen, the last being Jesus' Resurrection.

The fourteen traditional stations are as follows:

Jesus is sentenced to death
Jesus carries his cross
Jesus falls for the first time
Jesus meets his mother
Simon of Cyrene helps Jesus carry the cross
Veronica wipes Jesus' face
Jesus falls for the second time
Jesus meets the women of Jerusalem
Jesus falls for the third time
Jesus is stripped of his clothes
Jesus is nailed to the cross
Jesus dies on the cross
Jesus came down from the cross
Jesus is placed in the tomb

Each station is usually accompanied by a specific prayer and a meditation on the event being commemorated. Many churches have images or statues representing each station on their walls, and the faithful move from station to station reciting the prayers and meditating on each event. This is particularly common during the Lenten season, in preparation for Easter.

45. The Prayer of Saint Ephrem the Syrian

Used particularly during Lent in the Orthodox tradition, this prayer asks God to give a spirit of chastity, humility, patience and love.

Saint Ephrem the Syrian was a 4th-century saint and Father of the Church, known for his spiritual poetry. He wrote a large number of hymns, poems and sermons, and several prayers are attributed to him. One of the best known is the Prayer of Saint Ephrem, which is used in the liturgy of the Orthodox Church, particularly during the period of Great Lent.

Here is the text of this prayer:

"Lord and Master of my life, remove from me the spirit of laziness, discouragement, domination and empty words.

(monastic prostration or deep reverence)

But give your servant the spirit of chastity, humility, patience and love.

(monastic prostration or deep reverence)

Yes, Lord King, grant me to see my own faults and not to judge my brother, for You are blessed for ever and ever. Amen."

(monastic prostration or deep reverence)

The instructions in brackets indicate when to make these gestures during the prayer.

This prayer is often recited with a series of prostrations or deep reverences, symbolising humility before God. The prayer is recited focusing on the spirit of repentance and seeking God's mercy.

46. The Miserere (Psalm 51)

It is a prayer of repentance and of asking God for mercy.

The Miserere, also known as Psalm 51, is one of the penitential psalms in the Bible's Book of Psalms. Traditionally attributed to King David after the prophet Nathan confronted him about his adultery with Bathsheba, this psalm is a prayer of repentance and a plea for mercy from God. Here is the text of the psalm:

1 O God, be gracious to me according to your goodness,
According to the greatness of your compassion, blot out my transgressions!
2 Wash me thoroughly of my guilt,
And cleanse me of my sin.
3 For I am conscious of my transgressions,
And my sin is always before me.
4 Only you have I sinned against,
And I've done what's wrong in your eyes,
So that you will be just in your sentence,
Without reproach in your judgement.
5 See, I was born in sin,
And my mother conceived me in sin.
6 See, you want the truth to be inside a man;
Bring wisdom into my heart!
7 Purify me with hyssop, and I will be clean;
Wash me and I'll be whiter than snow.
8 Make me glad and rejoice,
And the bones you have broken will rejoice.
9 Look away from my sins,
Blot out all my iniquities.
10 O God, create in me a pure heart,
Renew in me a willing spirit.

11 Do not cast me away from your presence,
Don't take your holy spirit away from me.

12 Give me back the joy of your salvation,
And may a spirit of goodwill support me!

13 I will teach your ways to those who do them wrong,
And sinners will return to you.

14 O God, the God of my salvation,
Deliver me from bloodshed,
And my tongue will praise your mercy.

15 Lord, open my lips,
And my mouth will declare your praise.

16 If you had wanted sacrifices, I would have given them to
you;
But you have no pleasure in burnt offerings.
17 The sacrifices which are pleasing to God are a broken
spirit;
O God, you do not despise a broken and contrite heart.
18 Be gracious and pour out your blessings on Zion,
Build the walls of Jerusalem!
19 Then you will be happy with sacrifices of righteousness,
Holocausts and whole victims;
Then they will offer bulls on your altar.

This psalm is regularly used in Christian liturgies, particularly
during Lent and the penitential service.

47. The Prayer of Saint Catherine of Siena

A prayer asking for humility and love for God and others.

Saint Catherine of Siena was a 14th-century Dominican nun renowned for her piety and profound spirituality. She left numerous letters and a book, "The Dialogue", which contain many of her thoughts and prayers. Here is an example of a prayer attributed to Saint Catherine of Siena:

"Oh eternal love,

Eternal sweetness,

In your love, you carried us,

Poor and miserable,

Through your tenderness and your infinite love,

You made it come out of yourself,

These beautiful, gentle things,

And in your eternal love you have given them to us.

O love, who is always present to me

In the memory of your eternal sweetness,

Oh eternal love,

Eternal sweetness,

You are my refuge,

And my eternal love."

It is a prayer that focuses on God's eternal love for humanity and on the desire of the praying person to remain constantly in that love. It is a good illustration of the spirituality of Catherine of Siena, who dedicated her life to the love of God and charity towards her neighbour.

48. The Chaplet of Saint Anthony of Padua

Traditional prayer dedicated to Saint Anthony, the patron saint of lost objects.

The Chaplet of Saint Anthony of Padua is a specific form of prayer that uses a rosary dedicated to Saint Anthony. Saint Anthony of Padua, a 13th-century Franciscan priest, is known for his eloquent preaching and his particular devotion to the Infant Jesus. He is often invoked to find lost objects.

The rosary of Saint Anthony generally comprises thirteen groups of three beads each, representing the thirteen miracles attributed to Saint Anthony. A specific prayer is usually recited over each bead.

Here is an example of how the Chaplet of Saint Anthony might be recited:

On the cross of the rosary, we begin with the prayer of the Sign of the Cross: "In the name of the Father, and of the Son, and of the Holy Spirit. Amen."

On the first three beads, we recite an Our Father, a Hail Mary and a Glory be to the Father.

For each group of three beads, say :

On the first bead: "Saint Anthony, great servant of God, pray for us".

On the second bead: "Saint Anthony, friend of the Infant Jesus, pray for us".

On the third bead: "Saint Anthony, powerful miracle worker, pray for us".

At the end of the rosary, we recite the prayer of Saint Anthony: "O good and powerful Saint Anthony, always ready to help those who invoke your name, pray for us and grant us the grace to be always ready to serve God and our neighbour. Amen."

This is a way of praying that allows us to focus on the life and virtues of Saint Anthony, and to seek his intercession for our own needs.

49. The Regina Coeli (Queen of Heaven)

Marian prayer recited during the Easter season in place of the Angelus.

"Regina Coeli" or "Queen of Heaven" is an ancient hymn of the Catholic Church, sung in particular during the Easter season, from Easter to Pentecost, as a replacement for the Angelus. It is an expression of joy for the resurrection of Jesus Christ.

Here are the words of this prayer:

Queen of Heaven, rejoice, alleluia.

For he whom you have deserved to wear, alleluia,

Has risen, just as he said he would, hallelujah.

Pray to God for us, alleluia.

Be joyful and happy, Virgin Mary, alleluia,

For the Lord is truly risen, alleluia.

Let's pray.

O God, who by the resurrection of your Son, our Lord Jesus Christ, deigned to give joy to the world, grant us, through his Mother, the Virgin Mary, the joys of eternal life. Through Christ our Lord. Amen.

The singing of the Regina Coeli is a way for Christians to share in the Virgin Mary's joy at the resurrection of her son, and to implore her intercession.

50. The Prayer of Saint Bonaventure

A prayer asking God to help us find happiness in Him.

Saint Bonaventure, a 13th-century Franciscan theologian, left a large number of prayers and spiritual reflections. One notable example is his prayer for a spirit of devotion.

Here is a version of this prayer:

"Lord Jesus, plant your cross in me so that I may be protected by its power. May I take up my cross every day to follow you so that the old and sinful man in me may die. May I rise in you who are life and truth. Grant me, O Jesus, through the love of your cross, to disengage myself from the world and its seductions, and to renounce myself in order to follow you in poverty and humility. Grant that I may bear with patience the sorrows and adversities of this life for your sake. For you have said: If any man will be my disciple, let him deny himself, and take up his cross, and follow me. Amen."

It is a prayer that illustrates the spirituality of Saint Bonaventure, centred on Christ and the cross, self-denial and following him in everything.

51. The Prayer of Saint Ephrem

A prayer asking God to help us recognise our own faults and judge others charitably.

Saint Ephrem was a deacon, poet and theologian from fourth-century Syria. He is best known for his hymns and poems, which had a profound influence on the liturgy and spirituality of the Eastern Church. One of his best-known prayers is the "Prayer of Saint Ephrem the Syrian", often recited during Great Lent in the Eastern Orthodox Church.

"Lord and Master of my life, put away from me the spirit of laziness, discouragement, domination and vain words.

But give your servant the spirit of chastity, humility, patience and love.

Yes, Lord King, grant me to see my own faults and not to judge my brother, for You are blessed for ever and ever. Amen."

This prayer asks for God's help in combating vices and cultivating virtues, in particular humility and love.

52. The Chaplet of Divine Mercy

A prayer derived from the revelations of Saint Faustina Kowalska, asking God to exercise His mercy on us and on the whole world.

The Chaplet of Divine Mercy is a Catholic devotion focused on God's mercy, as revealed to Saint Faustina Kowalska. It is often recited using an ordinary rosary, but the prayers are specific to this devotion.

Here's how to pray the Chaplet of Divine Mercy:

Start by making the Sign of the Cross.

Then, on the first three beads of the rosary, recite an "Our Father", a "Hail Mary" and the "Apostles' Creed".

Then, over the large beads of the rosary, say the following prayer: "Eternal Father, I offer You the Body and Blood, Soul and Divinity of Your Beloved Son, our Lord Jesus Christ, in reparation for our sins and those of the whole world".

On the small beads, say: "Through his sorrowful Passion, be merciful to us and to the whole world".

Repeat these prayers for each decade of the rosary.

To conclude after the five decades, say three times, "Holy God, Strong God, Immortal God, have mercy on us and on the whole world."

And finally, say, "O eternal God, in the great misery of the whole world, may mercy come forth from the sanctuary to incline us to Thy omnipotent power, for if Thou dost not come to our aid, we are lost. Amen."

The Divine Mercy Chaplet is often recited as a novena (over nine consecutive days), particularly in the days leading up to the Feast of Divine Mercy, which is celebrated on the first Sunday after Easter.

53. The Prayer of Saint Thomas More

Prayer asking for God's help in maintaining integrity when faced with challenges.

Saint Thomas More, known as an English scholar, statesman and martyr, is famous for his piety and integrity. One of St Thomas More's best-known prayers is the one he wrote while imprisoned in the Tower of London, awaiting execution for refusing to renounce his Catholic faith.

Here is this prayer, entitled "The Prayer of Saint Thomas More in times of adversity":

"Lord, give me the grace to rejoice in the joy that is found only in You; not to be too absorbed by the fleeting things of this world. Give me the strength to resist the temptations of the evil one, and the wisdom to discern good from evil. Give me the will to correct and improve myself, not to judge others too harshly, but to love them as you love me. And when things don't go as I would like, give me the patience to bear the evils of this life, and perseverance in your service. Amen."

This prayer reflects the deep faith and resilience of St Thomas More in the face of adversity. It can be used by those going through difficult times or seeking to deepen their commitment to the Christian life.

54. The Te Deum

A hymn of thanksgiving dating from the 4th century, traditionally attributed to Saint Ambrose.

Te Deum is an ancient Christian hymn of praise and thanksgiving to God. Its name comes from the first Latin words of the hymn, "Te Deum laudamus", which means "God, we praise You". It is traditionally attributed to two 4th-century saints, Saint Ambrose and Saint Augustine, although its exact origin is not certain. The hymn is often used in Christian liturgies, particularly in praise services.

We praise You, O God,
we acknowledge You as Lord.
All the earth adores Your eternal majesty.
All the angels are Yours,
Thine are the heavens and all the powers,
To Thee the cherubim and seraphim sing without ceasing:
Holy, holy, holy is the Lord, God of the universe.
The heavens and the earth are full of Your glory.
The glorious choir of apostles,
The admirable number of prophets,
The white army of martyrs praise You.
Throughout the world, the Holy Church recognises You:
Father of infinite majesty,
Your one and only Son, worthy of all adoration,
And also the Holy Spirit, the Comforter.
You are the King of glory, O Christ.
You are the eternal Son of the Father.
When you took our weak nature to save man,
You were not averse to the Virgin Mary.
When You conquered death, You opened the kingdom of heaven to believers.

**You sit at the right hand of God, in the glory of the Father.
We believe that You will come to judge us.
So we pray You, help Your servants whom You have
redeemed with Your precious blood.
Bring them into the number of Your saints, into eternal
glory.**

This prayer is often recited or sung at special liturgical celebrations, such as ordinations or feasts of thanksgiving.

55. The Litanies of the Sacred Heart

Series of prayers addressed to the Sacred Heart of Jesus.

The Litanies of the Sacred Heart are a form of prayer in which the faithful invoke the Sacred Heart of Jesus several times, each invocation being followed by a standard response, often "Have mercy on us". Here is an example of one of these litanies:

Lord, have mercy on us.
Christ, have mercy on us.
Lord, have mercy on us.
Christ, listen to us.
Christ, hear us.

God, Father in heaven, have mercy on us.
God the Son, Redeemer of the world, have mercy on us.
God, the Holy Spirit, have mercy on us.
Holy Trinity, one God, have mercy on us.

Heart of Jesus, Son of the eternal Father, have mercy on us.
Heart of Jesus, formed by the Holy Spirit in the womb of the Virgin Mother, have mercy on us.
Heart of Jesus, united substantially to the Word of God, have mercy on us.
Heart of Jesus, of infinite majesty, have mercy on us.
Heart of Jesus, holy temple of God, have mercy on us.
Heart of Jesus, tabernacle of the Most High, have mercy on us.
Heart of Jesus, house of God and gateway to heaven, have mercy on us.
Heart of Jesus, burning furnace of charity, have mercy on us.
Heart of Jesus, shrine of justice and love, have mercy on us.

Heart of Jesus, full of goodness and mercy, have mercy on us.

And so on... There are many other invocations that can be included in the Litanies of the Sacred Heart, but they all follow the same pattern, invoking the Heart of Jesus and asking for his mercy. These litanies are often prayed during the month of June, which is traditionally dedicated to the Sacred Heart in the Catholic Church.

56. The Rosary of the Precious Blood

It is a devotion to Jesus Christ whose purpose is to honour the blood he shed for humanity and to ask for graces.

The Chaplet of the Precious Blood is a special form of devotion prayed on a rosary, focusing on the seven episodes in Christ's life where his Precious Blood was shed. This is how it is usually prayed:

1) Start with the sign of the cross.

2) Recite the invocation, "O Jesus, by your precious Blood which was shed in Gethsemane, have mercy on us and on the whole world."

3) On the large rosary, recite the Our Father.

4) On the small rosaries, recite: "Eternal Father, I offer you the Precious Blood of Jesus Christ, in atonement for my sins, for the good of the Church, the souls in Purgatory and the needs of all men".

5) Repeat steps 2 to 4 for the other six mysteries, changing the invocation to reflect each mystery of the Precious Blood :

- The scourging at the column ("O Jesus, by your precious Blood which was shed in the scourging, have mercy on us and on the whole world").
- The crowning of thorns ("O Jesus, by your precious Blood which was shed at the crowning of thorns, have mercy on us and on the whole world").

- The carrying of the Cross ("O Jesus, by your precious Blood which was shed during the carrying of the Cross, have mercy on us and on the whole world").
- The crucifixion ("O Jesus, by your precious Blood which was shed at the crucifixion, have mercy on us and on the whole world").
- The spear wound ("O Jesus, by your precious Blood which flowed from the spear wound, have mercy on us and on the whole world").

6) At the end of the rosary, recite three times: "O Eternal Father, have mercy on us through the Blood of Jesus, your only Son. O Precious Blood of Jesus, save us and the whole world."

7) Finish with the sign of the cross.

It is a prayer of great reparation and intercession, recommended especially in times of great personal, family, community and world need.

57. The Prayer of Saint Francis Xavier

This prayer is often recited to ask for the intercession of Saint Francis Xavier, a Jesuit missionary who worked to spread Christianity in Asia.

The Prayer of Saint Francis Xavier is a prayer of intercession and devotion addressed to this great saint, known for his missionary work in Asia. Here is a typical version of this prayer:

"Beloved Saint Francis Xavier, in your earthly life you showed tireless zeal for the glory of God and the salvation of souls, and you devoted all your energy to this mission. Today we ask you to intercede for us before the throne of God, so that we too may live out our vocation with the same dedication and love.

We pray to you in particular for (mention your special request here).

Through your powerful intercession, may we receive the graces we need to live the Gospel faithfully and serve God in our brothers and sisters.

Saint Francis Xavier, pray for us. Amen."

It is worth noting that the prayers of the saints can generally be personalised according to the specific needs of the person praying. This is why the insertion of a specific request is often included.

58. The Prayer of Saint Basil the Great

Saint Basil is one of the Church Fathers of the Eastern Orthodox tradition, and this prayer is a request for divine guidance and help.

Saint Basil the Great is renowned for his wisdom and deep love of God. His prayers reflect this passion. Here is one of his best-known prayers:

"O Lord and King of the universe, who art the creator of all things, heaven and earth, who art immeasurable and incomprehensible: Thou, Lord, teach me to fear Thee and adore Thee with all my heart and soul.

Teach me to repent sincerely of my sins and to pray fervently, so that I may receive You into my heart and feel Your holy presence.

Help me, Lord, to have an unshakeable faith in You, with the hope and love that go with that faith.

Give me the courage to follow You, who are the way, the truth and the life.

Finally, O Saviour, I pray and I beseech You, guide me so that by Your grace I may obtain the Kingdom of Heaven. Amen."

It is a prayer of repentance, adoration, request for guidance and strengthening of faith, addressed to God with Saint Basil as intercessor.

59. The Prayer of Saint Anselm

This prayer is a request for help in faith and an expression of desire for knowledge of God.

Saint Anselm of Canterbury is known for his contributions to theology and philosophy, and in particular for his ontological argument for the existence of God. Here is a prayer attributed to Saint Anselm:

"My soul, give thanks and love Him who loves you. My soul, give thanks to Him who, on this day, has done so much good for you, and for so many blessings received from Him, love God with all your heart.

Yes, Lord God, my Creator and my Saviour, for all the joy I have received from You, for all that You have done and are doing for me, may my soul bless You, and may everything in me give You thanks, O my God, my Lord.

Amen."

This prayer expresses gratitude for God's blessings and love for the Creator and Saviour.

60. The Prayer of the Heart

In the Eastern Orthodox tradition, the "Prayer of the Heart" or "Jesus Prayer" is a repetitive or meditative prayer consisting of a simple invocation of the name of Jesus.

The Prayer of the Heart is a meditative prayer widely used in the Eastern Orthodox Church. It is also known as the "Jesus Prayer". The aim of this prayer is to focus the mind and heart on the presence of God. This is how it is usually said:

"Lord Jesus Christ, Son of God, have mercy on me, a sinner."

It's a simple prayer, but a powerful one. Repeating it allows you to concentrate on God's presence and keep all distractions at bay. The aim is to pray this prayer constantly, making your whole life a prayer. This enables the person praying to remain in God's presence throughout the day.

61. The Magnificat

This is the Virgin Mary's canticle from the Gospel according to Saint Luke (1:46-55), in which she praises God for his marvellous deeds.

The Magnificat is a very important prayer in the Christian tradition. It is also called the Song of Mary because it is spoken by the Virgin Mary in response to the greeting of her cousin Elizabeth in the Gospel of Luke (1:46-55). The text is as follows:

"My soul praises the Lord,
My spirit rejoices in God, my Saviour!
He looked on his humble servant;
From now on, all ages will call me blessed.
The Mighty One did wonders for me;
Holy is his name!
His love extends from age to age
On those who fear him.
Deploying the strength of his arm,
It scatters the superb.
He topples the powerful from their thrones,
He lifts up the humble.
He fills the hungry with good things,
Send the rich away empty-handed.
He raises up Israel his servant,
He remembers his love,

The promise made to our fathers,
In favour of Abraham and his descendants for ever.

This prayer is used in both Catholic and Protestant worship, particularly as part of the Liturgy of the Hours.

62. The Benedictus

This is Zechariah's canticle from the Gospel according to Saint Luke (1:68-79), which thanks God for the coming of the Messiah.

The Benedictus, also known as the Song of Zechariah, is a prayer of praise and gratitude to God that appears in the Gospel of Luke (1:68-79). Zechariah, the father of John the Baptist, uttered this prayer after the birth of his son. He gives thanks to God for the liberation of Israel and prophesies his son's mission as the forerunner of Christ.

Here is the text of the prayer:

**"Blessed be the Lord, the God of Israel,
who visits and redeems his people.
He has brought forth the strength that saves us
in the house of David his servant,
as he had announced by the mouth of his saints,
through his prophets, from ancient times:
salvation that snatches us from the enemy,
at the hands of all our adversaries;
love he shows towards our fathers,
memory of his holy covenant,
oath sworn to our father Abraham
to surrender without fear,
so that, delivered from the hand of enemies,
we serve him in righteousness and holiness,
in his presence, throughout our days.
And you, little child, will be called a prophet of the Most High:
you will go before the Lord to prepare his ways,
to announce salvation to his people,
the remission of his sins.**

Through the tender compassion of our God,
the light from on high will dawn on us,
to illuminate those who dwell in darkness and the shadow
of death,
and lead our footsteps to the path of peace".

This prayer is part of the liturgy of the hours in the Catholic Church and is traditionally recited during the office of Lauds (morning prayers).

63. The Nunc Dimittis

Simeon's hymn from the Gospel according to Saint Luke (2:29-32), which gives thanks to God for the revelation of Christ as the light of the Gentiles.

The Nunc Dimittis, also known as the Song of Simeon, is a prayer from the Gospel of Luke (2:29-32). It is named after the first words of its Latin version, "Nunc dimittis servum tuum, Domine", which mean "Now, Lord, let your servant go in peace". Here is the text of the prayer:

"Now, O sovereign Master,

you can let your servant go

in peace, according to your word.

For my eyes have seen salvation

that you were preparing before the eyes of the people:

the light that reveals itself to the nations

and give glory to your people Israel."

In the context of the Gospel, Simeon was a just and pious man who had received a divine revelation that he would not die until he had seen the Messiah. When he saw the baby Jesus at his presentation in the Temple, he recognised him as the Saviour and prayed this prayer.

The Nunc Dimittis is often used in Christian worship, particularly in the liturgy of the hours, where it is usually recited during compline (the night prayers).

64. The Rosary of Saint Michael the Archangel

This prayer honours Saint Michael and the nine choirs of angels.

The Rosary of St Michael the Archangel is a devotion specific to the Catholic tradition. It was introduced by Blessed Anne Catherine Emmerick (1774-1824), a German Augustinian nun, mystic and stigmatic.

The Rosary of Saint Michael the Archangel consists of nine salutations, one for each choir of angels, and three closing prayers. The greetings are generally preceded by an "Our Father" and three "Hail Marys". Each greeting is followed by the recitation of a "Hail Mary" in honour of each angelic choir.

Here is an example of how this rosary could be recited:

1) **Through the intercession of Saint Michael and the heavenly choir of Seraphim, may the Lord make us worthy of being inflamed with perfect love for God. Amen. (Our Father, three Hail Marys)**

2) **Through the intercession of Saint Michael and the heavenly choir of Cherubim, may the Lord grant us the grace to abandon the ways of sin and follow the path of Christian perfection. Amen. (Our Father, three Hail Marys)**

[Continue in this way for the Thrones, Dominations, Powers, Virtues, Principalities, Archangels and Angels]

The closing prayers are then recited:

1) O Saint Michael, prince of angels and guide of souls to heaven, intercede for us with God, repel the attacks of evil and help us to rejoice with you and all the saints in the eternal glory of God. Amen.

2) May the Lord help us through the prayers of the Archangel Saint Michael and all the angels. We pray Amen.

3) And may eternal rest be granted to our deceased, through the intercession of Saint Michael the Archangel and all the angels. Amen.

It is a powerful devotion that recalls the angelic hierarchy and the importance of the intercession of angels in the Christian life.

65. The Prayer of Saint John Damascene

It is a prayer that asks for the intercession of the Mother of God.

Saint John Damascene (or Saint John of Damascus) was an 8th-century priest and theologian of the Church. He is best known for his vigorous defence of the cult of icons against the iconoclasts. He also wrote many hymns and prayers that are still used in the Orthodox Church today.

Here is one of his most famous prayers, known as the "Prayer of Saint John Damascene to the Theotokos" (the Mother of God):

"O most pure Virgin Mary, mother of God, queen of virgins, treasure of divine grace, hope of the hopeless and refuge of sinners, we turn to you because you are our help and our protector. You are the joy of the angels, the crowning glory of the saints, the salvation of the world and the only hope of our souls. We call on you in our afflictions and our sorrows. Be our safety in storms, our light in darkness, our consolation in sorrow, and our sweetest protection at the hour of death. Deliver us from every kind of evil and every danger. Grant that we may, after this life, attain eternal bliss, through the intercession of your beloved Son, Jesus Christ, our Lord and our God, who is worthy of all glory, honour and adoration, now and ever and unto ages of ages. Amen."

66. The Akathistos

In the Eastern Orthodox tradition, the Akathistos is a hymn in honour of the Mother of God.

The Akathistos, or Akathist, is a poetic prayer dedicated to a saint, a sacred event, or the Most Holy Mother of God in the Eastern Christian tradition, particularly the Orthodox tradition. The most famous Akathist is that dedicated to the Theotokos (Mother of God), and is often simply called "The Akathist".

The Akathist is divided into twenty-four stanzas, corresponding to the twenty-four letters of the Greek alphabet. Each stanza begins with a different letter of the alphabet, in alphabetical order.

Here is an extract from the Akathist to the Theotokos (approximate translation, the original being in Greek):

"Rejoice, you through whom joy will shine!
Rejoice, you, the redemption of Adam's kind!
Rejoice, for you have brought down the hard hearts of the devils!
Rejoice, you who gave birth to the Light, guide of hearts!
Rejoice, you who have put an end to the ancient curse!
Rejoice, you who gave birth to the Blessing!
Rejoice, source of incorruptible life!
Rejoice, you who make known the Kingdom of Heaven!"

The exact structure and words of the Akathist may vary according to local traditions and translations, but the essence of the prayer remains the same.

67. The Chaplet of the Divine Childhood

It is a special devotion to the childhood of Jesus.

The Chaplet of the Divine Childhood is a special prayer dedicated to Jesus in his infant form. It is a lesser-known devotion in Christianity, but nonetheless an important one for those seeking to draw closer to the innocence and simplicity of Christ's childhood.

Here's how to pray the Chaplet of the Divine Childhood:

1) Start with the sign of the cross.

2) Repeat three times: "Divine Child Jesus, listen to me, help me, answer me".

3) Recite the Ave Maria.

4) On the grains of the "Our Father", say: "Child Jesus, I trust in you".

5) On the grains of the "Hail Mary", say: "And Jesus, the divine Child, will grow in wisdom, age and grace, before God and man".

6) Continue repeating steps 4 and 5 for all the beads in the rosary.

7) To finish, repeat three times: "Divine Infant Jesus, listen to me, help me, answer me".

Please note that as with any devotion, the important thing is the intention and the heart with which you pray, rather than the exact words used.

68. The Prayer of Saint Thomas Aquinas after Communion

This prayer is often recited after the reception of the Eucharist and asks for God's help in remaining faithful to his promises.

The prayer of Saint Thomas Aquinas after communion is a well-known prayer in the Catholic tradition. Here is the text of this prayer:

"I thank You, holy Lord, almighty Father, eternal God, who deign to nourish me with the Body and Blood of Your Son Jesus Christ our Lord, through whom I am assured of receiving eternal life. Please grant that, having been thus nourished with the divine life here on earth, I may also deserve to be counted at table among the guests in heaven. You who live and reign for ever and ever. Amen."

This prayer expresses gratitude for the Eucharistic gift of Christ's body and blood, and hope in the eternal life promised by communion with God.

69. The Morning Prayer of Saint Philomena

This prayer asks for Saint Philomena's intercession for the day ahead.

Saint Philomena was a young martyr from the early 4th century. Her popularity grew in the 19th century after several miracles were attributed to her intercession. Her morning prayer is as follows:

"O glorious Saint Philomena, filled with love for God and neighbour, I turn to you in the hope of finding comfort and help. Accept my requests and my needs and present them to God. Through your intercession, may I receive the graces and favours I so much need in the trials, tribulations and sufferings of life, especially (mention your specific request here), and may I, like you, one day exult in the eternal glory of paradise. Amen."

Note: Specific prayers may vary slightly depending on the source and translation.

70. The Litany of Saint Joseph

These litanies invoke the intercession of Saint Joseph, the husband of the Virgin Mary and foster father of Jesus.

The Litany of Saint Joseph is a series of invocatory prayers addressed to Saint Joseph, the earthly father of Jesus Christ. They were approved by Pope Pius X in 1909. The litanies are usually recited after the rosary, particularly during the month of March, which is dedicated to Saint Joseph. Here is a version of the litanies:

"Lord, have mercy on us.
Christ, have mercy on us.
Lord, have mercy on us.
Christ, hear us.
Christ, listen to us.
God, Father in heaven, have mercy on us.
God the Son, Redeemer of the world, have mercy on us.
God, the Holy Spirit, have mercy on us.
Holy Trinity, one God, have mercy on us.

Saint Joseph, pray for us
Noble son of David, pray for us
Light of the Patriarchs, pray for us
Spouse of the Mother of God, pray for us
Chaste guardian of the Virgin, pray for us
Nurturing Father of the Son of God, pray for us
Zealous defender of Jesus, pray for us
Head of the Holy Family, pray for us
Most righteous Joseph, pray for us
Joseph, most chaste, pray for us
Joseph, very prudent, pray for us

Joseph, very courageous, pray for us
Most obedient Joseph, pray for us
Most faithful Joseph, pray for us
Mirror of patience, pray for us
Friend of poverty, pray for us
Model of the workers, pray for us
Glory to family life, pray for us
Guardian of virgins, pray for us
Family support, pray for us
Consolation of the unfortunate, pray for us
Hope for the sick, pray for us
Patron saint of the dying, pray for us
Terror of the demons, pray for us
Protector of the Holy Church, pray for us

Lamb of God, who takes away the sins of the world,
forgive us, Lord.
Lamb of God, who takes away the sins of the world,
hear us, O Lord.
Lamb of God, who takes away the sins of the world,
have mercy on us.

He made him master of his house
And steward of all his property

Let us pray,
God, who in your ineffable providence deigned to choose
Saint Joseph as the spouse of your most holy Mother, grant,
we pray you, that we may deserve to have as our intercessor
in heaven the one whom we venerate as our protector on
earth. You who live and reign for ever and ever. Amen."

71. The Holy Spirit Prayer of Saint Teresa of Avila

This prayer asks for the help of the Holy Spirit to live according to God's will.

The prayer to the Holy Spirit, often attributed to Saint Teresa of Avila, is in fact an anonymous prayer. It is a popular prayer in the Christian tradition and is often said at the opening of meetings or gatherings to invite the presence and inspiration of the Holy Spirit. Here is an example of this prayer:

"Come, Holy Spirit,
Fill the hearts of your faithful
And kindle in them the fire of your love.
Send forth your Spirit and all will be created.
And you will renew the face of the earth.

O God, who instructed the hearts of the faithful
By the light of the Holy Spirit,
Give us, by the same Spirit,
The understanding and love of justice,
And that, by the consolation of his inspiration,
We always enjoyed his consolations.
Through Christ our Lord.
Amen."

This prayer asks the Holy Spirit to come, to inspire, to give wisdom, love for what is right and to bring comfort.

72. Morning prayer to the Holy Trinity

This Eastern Orthodox prayer asks for the help of the Trinity for the day ahead.

The Morning Prayer to the Holy Trinity is an invocation addressed to God in his three Persons - the Father, the Son and the Holy Spirit - which Christians confess in the dogma of the Trinity. Here is an example of this prayer:

"O Holy Trinity, Father, Son and Holy Spirit, I adore You and give You thanks for all the blessings You showered on me last night. I offer You my thoughts, words, actions and sufferings of this day. May all things be done for Thy glory and according to Thy holy will. Amen."

This prayer, said on waking, helps to consecrate the coming day to the Holy Trinity. It reminds the faithful of God's constant presence and unconditional love.

73. The Litany of the Holy Cross

These litanies invoke the power of the cross of Jesus.

The Litany of the Holy Cross is a series of traditional Catholic prayers dedicated to the Holy Cross. In Catholic practice, litanies generally consist of a series of invocations or supplications addressed to God, the Virgin Mary or a specific saint.

Please note that the texts of the prayers may vary according to local traditions and different translations. Here is an example of the Litany of the Holy Cross:

Lord, have mercy on us.
Christ, have mercy on us.
Lord, have mercy on us.

Heavenly Father, who art God, have mercy on us.
Son, Redeemer of the world, who art God, have mercy on us.
Holy Spirit, who art God, have mercy on us.
Holy Trinity, you are one God, have mercy on us.

Holy Mary, pray for us.
Holy Mother of God, pray for us.
Blessed Virgin of virgins, pray for us.
You who have found the Holy Cross, pray for us.

Through the Holy Cross, deliver us, O Lord.

Through the passion and death of Jesus on the Cross, deliver us, O Lord.
Through his descent into hell, deliver us, O Lord.
Through his resurrection, deliver us, O Lord.

Through his ascension, deliver us, O Lord.
Through the coming of the Holy Spirit, the Paraclete, deliver us, O Lord.

Lord, deliver us on the day of judgement.

Sinners, we pray you, hear us.

So that you may spare us, Lord, we pray you, hear us.
So that you may forgive us, Lord, we pray you, hear us.

So that you may lead all Christians to true unity, we pray you, hear us.
So that you may guide us to a holy end, we pray you, hear us.

Lamb of God, who takes away the sins of the world, forgive us, O Lord.
Lamb of God, who takes away the sins of the world, hear us, O Lord.
Lamb of God, who takes away the sins of the world, have mercy on us.

V. Lord, do not treat us according to our sins.
R. And do not punish us for our iniquities.

Let's pray,
God, who by the passion of your Son, our Lord, destroyed death, the ancient inheritance of sin by the first man; we pray that by devotion to the Holy Cross we may obtain eternal life. Through the same Jesus Christ, our Lord. Amen.

74. Saint Augustine's Prayer to the Holy Trinity

This prayer expresses deep admiration for the mystery of the Trinity.

Saint Augustine's prayer to the Holy Trinity is a beautiful invocation that emphasises divine love and the quest for God. Here is the text of this prayer:

"O eternal and true Trinity, O eternal and true Divinity, sweet and lovable! You who created everything in your image and likeness, may I always remember you, may I always understand you, may I always love you. May I always be as you wanted me to be for your glory. May I always serve you in your love.

O loving Father!

O Word, all lovable!

O Spirit, all lovable!

All-loving Trinity, you my true God!

O Divine Trinity, my Creator and my Saviour! You who are all my wealth and happiness, my joy and bliss, my hope and glory, grant me, through your mercy, whatever pleases you. Amen."

75. The Prayer of Saint François de Sales

This prayer asks for the intercession of Saint François de Sales in order to lead a life of devotion.

Saint François de Sales, bishop of Geneva in the 17th century, is known for his deep faith and his spiritual writings. Here is an example of a prayer by Saint François de Sales, also known as "Abandonment to Divine Providence":

"My God, I don't know what's going to happen to me today,

but I know that nothing will happen to me that you haven't planned and ordered for my greater good.

So I accept you now and in advance, with a joyful and tranquil heart,

for anything you do or send me.

I accept you, my God, because you are infinitely wise and infinitely powerful,

infinitely good, I love you and want everything you want, I want everything the way you want it,

I want everything to please you, I want everything with your grace, Amen."

76. The Rosary of the Virgin Mary

This is a Marian devotion that includes meditation on the "mysteries" or events in the lives of Jesus and Mary.

The Rosary of the Virgin Mary, also known as the Rosary, is a form of repetitive prayer that involves reciting several prayers while meditating on "mysteries" or events in the lives of Jesus and Mary. Here's how it's usually done:

1)Make the sign of the cross and say the Apostolic Creed (I believe in God).

2) Say the Lord's Prayer.

3) Say three Hail Marys.

4) Say Glory to the Father.

5) Announce the first mystery; then say the Our Father.

6) Say ten Hail Marys, meditating on the mystery.
7) Say Glory to the Father.
8) Announce the second mystery; say the Our Father. Repeat steps 6 and 7 and continue with the third, fourth and fifth mysteries in the same way.
9)Say the Salve Regina.
10)Make the sign of the cross.

There are four series of Mysteries: the Joyful Mysteries, the Luminous Mysteries, the Sorrowful Mysteries and the Glorious Mysteries. Normally, one series of Mysteries is prayed each day.

77. The Prayer of Saint Clare of Assisi

This prayer asks for the intercession of Saint Clare, a disciple of Saint Francis.

The prayer of Saint Clare of Assisi is an example of Christian devotion that inspires peace and love for God. Clare of Assisi was a disciple of Saint Francis of Assisi and founded the Order of Poor Clares, also known as "The Poor Ladies". Here is an example of a prayer attributed to St Clare:

"O most glorious God, enlighten the darkness of my heart.

Give me an upright faith, a sure hope and perfect charity.

Give me sense and knowledge, Lord,

So that I may fulfil your holy and true commandment. Amen."

78. The Evening Prayer of Saint Brigid

This prayer asks for God's protection during the night.

The Evening Prayer of Saint Brigid is a prayer of devotion and protection. Saint Brigid is an important figure in Christian history, being the co-patroness of Ireland and the founder of the Order of the Brigittines. Here is an example of Saint Brigid's evening prayer:

"O Lord, guide us in your eternal ways.

Protect us this night,

and in all the nights of this earthly life.

Preserve us from all evil,

from all danger and worry.

May your blessing hand rest upon us.

May your gentle light illuminate our dreams,

and may your love envelop our hearts.

We ask this through Jesus Christ,

our Lord and Saviour. Amen."

79. The Act of Hope

It is a prayer that expresses deep trust in God's promises and the hope of eternal life.

The Act of Hope is a traditional Christian prayer expressing deep faith and hope in God's mercy and Christ's promises. Here is an example of this prayer:

"My God, I hope with firm confidence that you will give me, through the merits of Jesus Christ, your grace in this world and eternal happiness in the next, because you promised it and you are faithful to keep your promises. Amen."

80. Prayer of Saint Monica

She is known for her persistent prayers for the conversion of her son, Saint Augustine.

The prayer of Saint Monica, often invoked by parents worried about their children, is not formally defined in the liturgical texts. However, a traditional prayer is often addressed to her:

"Saint Monica, you who obtained from God the conversion of your son, Saint Augustine, we entrust our children to you. You know our concern for them. How much we desire their happiness, but we cannot do everything. Pray for them! Pray for us! May we have the joy of seeing them happy on this earth and in eternity. Amen."

Saint Monica's prayer reminds us of the importance of perseverance in prayer. Even if we are sometimes tempted to become discouraged in the face of difficulties, we must remember that God hears our prayers and responds to our love and unshakeable faith. Like Saint Monica, let us continue to pray for those we love, ever hopeful of God's mercy and unconditional love. Amen.

81. Saint Alphonsus de Liguori's prayer to Jesus Crucified

A meditation on Jesus' suffering on the cross.

Saint Alphonsus de Liguori's prayer to Jesus Crucified is a cry from the heart filled with passion and devotion. Saint Alphonsus de Liguori was an 18th-century Catholic bishop, writer and moralist theologian who was canonised for his deep devotion and love for Christ. His prayer is a magnificent testimony to that love and a wonderful profession of faith. Here is the prayer:

"O my beloved Crucified One, O my Redeemer! You died for me on the Cross to draw me to your love. I would like, yes I would like to die of love for You who were willing to die of love for me. O my Lord! I don't want to live a single moment without loving you. O Jesus my love, I love you, I love you! O my Redeemer, help me, don't let me offend you again, and don't let me live a single moment without loving you. O love, O love, O love of Jesus, be my love for ever. So be it. Amen."

This deep and devoted prayer is a beautiful testimony to love for Jesus and an example of how faith can guide and nourish the soul. By meditating on these words, we are invited to draw closer to Christ and to deepen our own love and devotion to Him.

82. Saint Bernard of Clairvaux's prayer to the Virgin Mary (Memorare)

A powerful prayer invoking the intercession of the Virgin Mary.

Saint Bernard's prayer to the Virgin Mary, also known as "Memorare" (Remember), is a deeply moving invocation dedicated to Mary, mother of Jesus. Saint Bernard of Clairvaux, the great 12th-century theologian and Doctor of the Church, is renowned for his devotion to the Virgin Mary. Here is the prayer:

"Remember, O most merciful Virgin Mary,
we've never heard of
that someone has invoked your protection,
implored your assistance
or asked for your intercession,
and that it has been abandoned.
Encouraged by this confidence,
I come to you, O Virgin of virgins, O my Mother.
To you I come, before you I stand, sinful and sad.
O Mother of the Incarnate Word,
do not despise my prayers,
but listen to them favourably and deign to hear them.
Amen."

The "Memorare" reminds us of the tenderness, mercy and comfort that Mary can bring to our lives, while asking for her intercession in our times of need.

83. Prayer of Saint Rita of Cascia

She is known as the saint of desperate and impossible causes.

Saint Rita of Cascia, known as the saint of lost and desperate causes, is a popular devotional figure in the Catholic Church. Born in Italy in the 14th century, she led a life dedicated to prayer and service to others despite many personal trials. Here is a prayer addressed to Saint Rita:

"O Saint Rita, you who knew how to love without measure, intercede for me with God. Give me the strength to love my neighbour, even when he has done me wrong. Give me the patience to endure my trials and perseverance in prayer.

O Saint Rita, you who knew how to keep the faith in all circumstances, intercede for me with God. Help me to grow in faith, hope and charity. Give me the strength to forgive those who have offended me and guide me towards reconciliation and peace.

O Saint Rita, you who forgave those who killed your husband and sons, intercede for me with God. Make me an instrument of his peace. May I always know how to show love where there is hatred, forgiveness where there is offence, union where there is discord.

O Saint Rita, you who suffered illness and pain with courage, intercede for me with God. Give me the grace to bear life's sufferings with patience and courage, and to offer them for the conversion of sinners.

O Saint Rita, you who entered the convent despite all the

obstacles, intercede for me with God. Give me the strength to follow God's will in all things and always seek his glory and the good of my brothers.

O Saint Rita, pray for me and for all those who entrust themselves to your intercession. Amen."

This prayer reflects the spirit of forgiveness, perseverance, faith and love of neighbour that Saint Rita showed throughout her life. It can be of great comfort to those facing difficulties or desperate trials.

84. Saint John Bosco's prayer to Mary Help of Christians

A prayer asking for help from Mary, the Mother of God.

Saint John Bosco, also known as Don Bosco, was a 19th-century Italian priest and educator who dedicated his life to the education of disadvantaged young people. He had a great devotion to the Virgin Mary, whom he called Mary Help of Christians. Here is a prayer he composed in her honour:

"O Mary, mighty Virgin,

A great and illustrious defender of the Church,

Singular assistance from Christians,

Terrifying as an army arrayed in battle,

You alone have destroyed all heresy throughout the world,

In our distress, in our struggles,

In our anguish, protect us from the devil,

At the hour of death, welcome us to heaven. Amen."

This prayer highlights the strength and comfort that Saint John Bosco found in his devotion to Mary. He invoked her protection in times of struggle and anguish, and saw her as a defender of the Church and a helper of Christians.

85. Prayer of Saint Julienne of Norwich

A prayer of trust and faith in God's goodness.

Saint Julian of Norwich, also known as Dame Julian or Mother Julian, was a 14th-century English anchorite. She is best known for her book "Revelations of Divine Love", which is based on a series of visions she had and focuses on God's love and how it manifests itself in everyday life.

One of the best-known prayers attributed to Saint Juliana is the following:

"Almighty God, father of all mercies and consolations, you always regenerate your faithful with the heavenly sacraments: grant to your servant [insert name], that my illness may increase in him (or her) the fruits of good works. Through Jesus Christ our Lord. Amen."

Note that this prayer is often used in times of illness or distress, asking for divine intervention and comfort.

86. Saint Maximilian Kolbe's prayer to the Immaculate Conception

He offered everything to the Virgin Mary so that she could use it according to her good pleasure to accomplish God's will.

Saint Maximilian Kolbe was a Polish Catholic priest who gave his life for another prisoner in a concentration camp during the Second World War. He had a special devotion to the Virgin Mary. Here is an example of his prayer to the Immaculate:

"O Immaculate, Queen of Heaven and earth, refuge of sinners and most loving Mother to whom God wished to entrust the whole order of mercy, I am an unworthy sinner and I throw myself at your feet. I implore you through the Heart of Jesus, your dear Son, on behalf of all of us poor sinners, and in particular for those who are now in their agony and who will die today.

Most loving Mother, since you are here beside their deathbed, make all poor sinners a sincere act of contrition, and as Mother of Mercy, ask your divine Son to forgive them all their faults, so that they may leave this life in the sweet embrace of your eternal love. Amen."

87. Prayer of Saint Hildegard of Bingen

This prayer asks God to give us the strength to serve with sincere devotion.

Saint Hildegard of Bingen was a Benedictine abbess, composer, philosopher, mystic, visionary and writer of the 12th century. She left a lasting influence on church music and theology. Here is an example of her prayer:

"O gentle fire, in tranquillity, you are resplendent,

and most of all, in all purity, you are alive,

the wisdom of divine wisdom.

You are the radiance of eternal glory,

the spotless mirror of God's activity

and the image of his goodness.

Amen."

88. Saint John Paul II's prayer to Mary

A popular prayer to Mary written by Pope John Paul II.

Here is Saint John Paul II's prayer to Mary, also known as "Totus Tuus":

"Totus Tuus ego sum, et omnia mea Tua sunt.

Accipio Te in mea omnia. Praebe mihi cor Tuum, Maria (I am all yours, and all that I have is yours. I take you in all that is mine. Give me your heart, Mary.)

This prayer is a perfect illustration of Saint John Paul II's deep devotion to the Virgin Mary. "Totus Tuus" was in fact his episcopal motto, meaning "all yours". He dedicated his life and his pontificate to Mary, and this prayer is a fine example of his love and devotion to her.

89. Saint Jerome's prayer for the study of Scripture

A prayer for God's help in studying the Bible.

Saint Jerome's prayer for the study of Scripture is as follows:

"Lord, inspire me in love with your word; open my eyes so that I may see the wonders of your Law. Speak to my heart, and let my heart respond to you. Amen."

Saint Jerome is best known for translating the Bible into Latin, a version known as the Vulgate. In this prayer, he asks God to help him understand and love the Scriptures, so that he can better know and serve God.

90. Prayer of Saint Gertrude for the souls in Purgatory

This prayer is reputed to free a thousand souls from purgatory each time it is said.

Saint Gertrude's prayer for the souls in Purgatory is as follows:

"Eternal Father, I offer You the Most Precious Blood of Your Divine Son Jesus, in union with the Masses said today throughout the world, for all the holy souls in purgatory, for sinners everywhere, for sinners in the universal Church, those in my own home and family. Amen."

Saint Gertrude the Great was a Benedictine nun, theologian and mystic of the 13th century. She is best known for her writings on devotion to the Sacred Heart of Jesus and for her dedication to praying for the souls in purgatory. In the prayer above, she offers the sacrifice of Jesus to God the Father for the salvation of souls in purgatory, sinners in the world and in the Church, and even those in her own family.

91. Prayer of Saint Margaret Mary Alacoque to the Sacred Heart of Jesus

A devotional prayer to the Sacred Heart of Jesus.

The prayer of Saint Margaret Mary Alacoque to the Sacred Heart of Jesus is as follows:

"O Sacred Heart of Jesus, to you I have recourse; in you I find my consolation when afflicted I am pursued; in you I find my strength when weak I am burdened; in you I have my refuge when fear overwhelms me. O sacred heart of Jesus, be my refuge and my strength; defend me from all the attacks of my enemies. I consecrate my actions to you so that I may do them according to your holy will. Amen."

Saint Margaret Mary Alacoque is famous for having had several visions of Christ in which he revealed his Sacred Heart to her. She played an important role in establishing devotion to the Sacred Heart of Jesus in the Catholic Church. This prayer expresses total trust in and dependence on the Sacred Heart of Jesus, a source of comfort, strength and protection. It also pledges to act according to God's will, dedicating all one's actions to the Sacred Heart.

92. Prayer of Saint John of the Cross

A prayer asking God to purify her soul so that she can better serve and love Him.

The prayer of Saint John of the Cross, an important figure of the Counter-Reformation and a Spanish mystic, is as follows:

"O Lord, my God, who are infinitely lovable above all things, may I love you with all my heart, may I desire you with all my soul, may I adore you in the depths of my being! May nothing distract my attention from you, may nothing disturb my peace in you, may you alone be my joy, my desire and my consolation, may you alone always be in my thoughts and in my heart, day and night, and may I always remain patient, generous, humble and gentle towards my neighbour for your sake. Amen."

This prayer expresses a deep love for God and a desire to remain centred on Him, despite life's distractions and difficulties. Saint John of the Cross also expresses a desire to live Christian virtues, such as patience, generosity, humility and gentleness, in response to God's love.

93. Saint Benedict's prayer for seeking God

A prayer asking God to help her seek His presence in everything.

The prayer of Saint Benedict, known for his great wisdom and love of God, is as follows:

"O good Father, you who see in secret, you know that I love you and that I want to love you more. Increase this love in me, so that my desire may be fulfilled in your presence. Grant that I may never seek to please men but only you, that I may be docile to your will, that I may obey you in everything, that I may renounce myself, take up my cross and follow you, my Lord and my God. May I be firm and constant, gentle and humble, patient and kind, full of faith, hope and love. Amen."

In this prayer, Saint Benedict asks God to help him to concentrate on Him rather than on the desires of the world, to be docile to His will, to renounce his personal ego and to follow God. He also asks God to help him develop the virtues of faith, hope and charity. This prayer expresses great devotion and a yearning for a deeper relationship with God.

94. Prayer of Saint Cecilia

Saint Cecilia is a martyr of the Roman Catholic Church, traditionally venerated as the patron saint of musicians. According to tradition, she sang praises to God even while being persecuted for her faith. Even today, she is invoked by those who seek to honour God through music.

The following prayer is an invocation to Saint Cecilia:

"Saint Cecilia, patron saint of music, who by your praise drew heaven to earth, guide our hands and voices so that our hearts may always be attuned to the praise of God.

Almighty God, through the intercession of Saint Cecilia, hear our prayers for the grace of true harmony, both in our own lives and in the symphony of your love for us. Make us your instruments and let our music resound to your glory.

May our souls be filled with your divine music, and may our love for you grow with every note we play and every song we sing. Saint Cecilia, pray for us."

In praying this prayer, we ask Saint Cecilia to help us align our lives with divine harmony, to use our musical talents for the glory of God, and to feel God's presence in our music and praise. We ask her to guide our creativity and devotion, so that our love for God is strengthened through our music.

95. Prayer of Saint Thomas de Villeneuve for charity towards the poor

A prayer asking God to help him be generous towards those in need.

Saint Thomas de Villeneuve, Archbishop of Valencia in Spain in the 16th century, is renowned for his deep charity and concern for the poor and needy. He is celebrated for giving generously of all he possessed to help those in need.

Here is a prayer attributed to Saint Thomas de Villeneuve which illustrates his great charity towards the poor:

"Lord, when I am hungry, give me someone who needs food. When I am thirsty, send me someone who needs water. When I'm cold, send me someone to warm me. When I am wounded, give me someone to care for. When my burden weighs heavily on my shoulders, give me the burden of others to carry. When I am poor, lead me to someone in need. When I have no time, give me someone I can help for a while. When I'm humiliated, give me someone to praise. When I'm discouraged, send me someone to encourage."

This prayer expresses a deep desire to see Jesus in the poor and to serve them with love and compassion, echoing the teachings of Jesus in the New Testament. In praying this prayer, we are invited to follow the example of Saint Thomas de Villeneuve and to look for opportunities for charity towards the poor in our own lives.

96. Saint Vincent de Paul's prayer for love of neighbour

A prayer asking God to help him love his neighbour as himself.

Saint Vincent de Paul is one of the emblematic figures of charity in the Catholic Church. Founder of the Congregation of the Mission and the Daughters of Charity, he devoted his life to serving the poor, the sick and the abandoned.

The following prayer expresses the essence of his spirituality, centred on love of neighbour:

"O Lord, instil in us the love, humility and poverty of your Son, Jesus. We ask you to help us serve our brothers and sisters in need with compassion and generosity. May our service be a witness to your love for all the men and women you have created. We ask this grace of you, Lord, through the intercession of Saint Vincent de Paul, your faithful servant."

In reciting this prayer, we ask God to help us imitate Jesus' love for all people, especially those in need, by following the example of Saint Vincent de Paul. This prayer reminds us that true love of neighbour goes beyond words and manifests itself in concrete acts of service and generosity towards those in need.

97. Prayer of Saint Jean-Marie Vianney

This prayer is a request for the intercession of the patron saint of priests.

Saint Jean-Marie Vianney, better known as the Curé d'Ars, is one of France's most famous saints. He is known for his deep piety, his devotion to confession and his love for souls.

Here is one of his prayers:

"My God, I offer you all the acts I am going to do today, in the intentions and for the glory of your sacred Heart. I want to sanctify every beat of my heart, every thought, my simplest actions, by uniting them to his infinite merits; and I want to make reparation for my sins by throwing them into the furnace of his merciful love."

By reciting this prayer, we commit ourselves to offering our actions of the day to God, to sanctifying them by uniting them to the merits of Jesus, and to seeking his forgiveness for our faults. It is a constant reminder of God's infinite mercy and the redeeming power of his love. In this way, this prayer can help us to start each day with a spiritual perspective and stay focused on our ultimate goal, which is union with God.

98. Prayer of Saint Anthony of Padua

Known as a prayer of intercession for lost objects.

Saint Anthony of Padua is one of the most beloved saints of the Catholic Church, renowned for helping to find lost objects and considered the patron saint of the poor. He is also known for his great erudition and eloquence as a preacher.

Here is a prayer attributed to Saint Anthony of Padua:

"Saint Anthony, you who have the power to recover what has been lost, help me to rediscover God's grace. Guide me to righteousness, purity and holiness. Inspire me to seek first the kingdom of God and his justice, knowing that God, who sees in secret, will reward."

This prayer calls on us to ask Saint Anthony's help not only to recover what has been lost in the material sense, but also to find our spiritual path when we have gone astray. It reminds us that our ultimate goal is to seek God's kingdom and his justice, and encourages us to live a life of righteousness, purity and holiness. May this prayer inspire you to constantly seek God's grace in your life.

99. Prayer of Saint Martin of Tours

This prayer is generally said to ask for Saint Martin's intercession on behalf of the poor and needy.

Saint Martin of Tours is one of the best-known and most venerated saints in Europe. He is best known for sharing his cloak with a beggar on a cold winter's night. Saint Martin also served as Bishop of Tours, France, and is known for his humility and devotion to the poor.

Here is a prayer in honour of Saint Martin of Tours:

"Saint Martin, you who showed the way to love and compassion, help me to follow in your footsteps. Give me a generous heart to serve the needy and abandoned, a strong will to overcome difficulties and challenges, and an unshakeable faith in divine providence. May I always be ready to share what I have with those who have less, as you shared your cloak with the beggar. Amen."

This prayer invites us to seek Saint Martin's intercession in our efforts to live a life of love, generosity and service to those less fortunate. It also reminds us that, just as Saint Martin had the faith to share his cloak in the knowledge that God would provide for his needs, so too should we have the faith to help others in trust of God's providence. May the example of Saint Martin inspire us to live the Gospel more fully in our daily lives.

100. Prayer of Saint Catherine of Siena

It is a prayer that asks for help in remaining firm in the faith and devoted to God.

Saint Catherine of Siena is one of the great mystics and doctors of the Church. She lived in 14th-century Italy and is renowned for her profound devotion and commitment to the reform of the Church. Known for her dialogue with God, she left behind a large number of letters and prayers. The following prayer is one of those attributed to Saint Catherine of Siena:

"O Eternal Lord, Light without light,
The sun that never sets,
Please enlighten me;
And warm me, most loving Father,
Because I'm cold and blind.
When I have you as my guide and support,
I will no longer fear the night or the thief,
For you are my way, the truth and the life.
In your light I will see the light,
And in your truth I'll find freedom,
And in your life, I'll be living the real life,
Eternally. Amen."

May this deeply spiritual and introspective prayer of Saint Catherine of Siena guide us towards a greater understanding of our own faith and inspire us to constantly seek light, truth and life in our relationship with God.

Printed in Great Britain
by Amazon

33391326R00076